TIME-LIFE FAVORITE RECIPES

QUICK MEALS

TIME
LIFE
BOOKS

Alexandria, Virginia

Time-Life Books is a division of Time Life Inc.

TIME LIFE INC.
PRESIDENT AND **CEO:** George Artandi

TIME-LIFE CUSTOM PUBLISHING
Vice President and Publisher: Terry Newell
Vice President of Sales and Marketing: Neil Levin
Director of Special Sales: Liz Ziehl
Editor for Special Markets: Anna Burgard
Production Manager: Carolyn Bounds
Quality Assurance Manager: James D. King
Pre-press Services: Time-Life Imaging Center

SPECIAL CONTRIBUTORS
Editing: Betty Bianconi, In Good Taste
Design: Anna Burgard
Design Production: Ruth Thompson,
Thunder Hill Graphics
Proofreading: Celia Beattie
Index: Judy Davis

This book is an adaptation of the Time-Life
series *Creative Everyday Cooking* © 1990

First printing. Printed in China

Time-Life is a trademark of Time Warner Inc.
U.S.A.

ISBN: 0-7370-1119-X

CIP data available upon application:
Librarian, Time-Life Books
2000 Duke Street
Alexandria, Virginia 22314

Books produced by Time-Life Custom Publishing are
available at special bulk discount for promotional and
premium use. Custom adaptations can also be creat-
ed to meet your specific marketing goals. Call 1-800-
323-5255

TABLE OF CONTENTS

Introduction   4

Poultry Dishes   6

Meat Dishes   28

Seafood and Fish   48

Beans and Vegetables   68

Metric Conversions   93

Index   94

INTRODUCTION

YOU CAN EAT WELL without wearing yourself out in the kitchen! Your schedule is packed, you juggle multiple activities and responsibilities in a world that never seems to slow down, and you're trying to feed your family, too. Maybe you think it's impossible to whip up good meals from scratch in the few minutes available. Maybe you're tired of preparing and eating expensive, packaged foods. Or, maybe you're exhausting yourself trying to cook that perfect meal with complicated recipes that have you running to the store for special ingredients.

It doesn't have to be that way. You can prepare delicious, nutritious food, made from simple ingredients, in a few easy steps. This handy book will help you discover 100 new, exciting ways to make a good meal without having to spend lots of time, buy exotic ingredients or learn complicated preparation techniques that take you out of your daily routine. These simple, easy-to-follow recipes range from basic fare like Stovetop Barbecued Burgers, Chicken Noodle Soup, and Spaghetti and Little Meatballs to elegant dishes like Spring Lamb and Asparagus Salad, Pecan Crusted Snapper or Simple Beef Burgundy.

The editors of Time-Life Books show you how to make great meals in a jiffy. Most dishes can be prepared with a few steps in under thirty minutes, so even after a busy day you can have a tempting and healthful meal. Each recipe is accompanied by nutritional information, such as fat, sodium, and protein content, so you know what you're feeding your family. There are handy preparation and serving tips, and of course, beautiful full-color photos of many of the dishes. And the book lies flat, so you won't have to keep rummaging to find your place.

Time Life Favorite Recipes: Quick Meals takes you from hearty soups and fresh, tasty salads through a variety of main course dishes. Try international or regional favorites like Chinese Hot Pot, South-of-the-Border Black Bean Soup, Fettuccine Alla Carbonara, or a simple Spanish Omelet. Learn to prepare classics like Modern Minestrone or Pesto with Linguine. In the mood for something cool and light? Serve Summer Turkey Salad, Greek Green Bean Salad, or Tuna Rice Salad. Want something warm to fill you up? Cook up a hearty Chicken and Tiny Star Pasta Stew, Microwave Baked Potato Stroganoff, or Salisbury Steaks with Savory Sauce. Hungry for a dish with some zest? How about Spicy Fajita Roll-Ups, Moroccan-Spiced Chicken Salad or Pork Chops Diablo? For a change of pace, try Broccoli and Ricotta Pizza, Chicken Parmesan Sandwiches, or Bean Burritos.

You'll find that after using this book you'll have a whole new list of favorites to fall back on! So go ahead and treat yourself and your family to a whole new world of eating—the quick and easy way!

POULTRY DISHES

Gingered Turkey Kebabs

Make these kebabs ahead and slip them into pita pockets
or hero rolls for a quick portable picnic.

Serves 4

3	SLICES ¼-INCH-THICK FRESH GINGER, MINCED
2	CLOVES GARLIC, MINCED
¼	CUP REDUCED-SODIUM SOY SAUCE
1	TABLESPOON ORIENTAL SESAME OIL
2	TEASPOONS CIDER VINEGAR
½	TEASPOON HONEY
¼	TEASPOON PEPPER
¾	POUND TURKEY SCALLOPINI, CUT LENGTHWISE INTO 1-INCH-WIDE STRIPS
1	LARGE ZUCCHINI, HALVED LENGTHWISE, CUT INTO 1-INCH CHUNKS
1	LARGE YELLOW PEPPER, CUT INTO 1-INCH PIECES
24	CHERRY TOMATOES
1	TEASPOON SESAME SEEDS

1 In shallow dish, combine ginger, garlic, soy sauce, sesame oil, vinegar, honey and pepper. Add turkey strips; toss to evenly coat. Let stand.

2 Preheat broiler. Line broiler pan with foil.

3 On each of 12 skewers weave equal amounts of turkey strips around zucchini, yellow pepper and tomatoes.

4 Place on broiler pan; brush with any remaining marinade. Sprinkle with sesame seeds. Broil 4 inches from heat source, turning once, until turkey is cooked through, about 6 to 8 minutes.

PREPARATION TIP

Place the turkey and marinade in a plastic bag up to a day ahead; then cut the vegetables and thread them just before eating for an easy 15-minute preparation-to-table meal.

Calories: 173 · Protein: 23 g
Fat: 5 g/26% Calories from Fat · Carbohydrate: 9 g
Cholesterol: 53 mg · Sodium: 665 mg

Chicken Tortilla Soup

The full flavor of the chicken is preserved by broiling the chicken separately and adding it to the rich tomato-based broth.

Serves 4

1	MEDIUM ONION, COARSELY CHOPPED
3	CLOVES GARLIC, MINCED
⅓	CUP FINELY CHOPPED CILANTRO
1	TABLESPOON PLUS 2 TEASPOONS OIL
1½	TEASPOONS DRIED OREGANO
½	TEASPOON PEPPER
½	POUND SKINLESS, BONELESS CHICKEN BREASTS
2	CUPS CHICKEN BROTH
1	CUP WATER
1	CAN (14½ OUNCES) NO-SALT-ADDED STEWED TOMATOES
1	CUP TOMATO JUICE
2	TEASPOONS GRATED LIME ZEST
2	TABLESPOONS LIME JUICE
½	TEASPOON WORCESTERSHIRE SAUCE
2	TEASPOONS CUMIN
1	FRESH OR PICKLED JALAPEÑO PEPPER, SEEDED AND MINCED
4	SMALL CORN TORTILLAS, CUT INTO CROSSWISE STRIPS, TOASTED
½	CUP SHREDDED MONTEREY JACK CHEESE (2 OUNCES)

1 Preheat broiler. In small bowl, combine half the onion, garlic and cilantro. Stir in the 1 tablespoon oil, ½ teaspoon of the oregano and ¼ teaspoon pepper.

2 Place chicken on broiler pan and top with onion-herb mixture. Broil 4 inches from heat source, 7 minutes.

3 Turn; baste with any pan juices and broil until cooked through, about 7 to 9 minutes. Cool; pull apart into shreds.

4 Meanwhile, in a medium saucepan, heat the remaining 2 teaspoons oil over medium-high heat.

5 Add the remaining onion and garlic; cook, stirring, until the onion is lightly browned, about 3 to 4 minutes.

6 Add broth, water, tomatoes, tomato juice, lime zest and juice, Worcestershire sauce and remaining cilantro, oregano and pepper and cumin.

7 Bring to a boil and reduce heat to low; cover and simmer 7 minutes. Stir in jalapeño.

8 To serve, ladle soup into bowls and top with chicken, tortilla strips and cheese.

PREPARATION TIP
To toast tortilla strips, place on baking sheet and bake in preheated 400° oven until toasted, about 7 minutes.

Calories: 343 · Protein: 22 g
Fat: 17 g/44% calories from Fat · Carbohydrate: 27 g
Cholesterol: 45 mg · Sodium: 1,151 mg

Chicken Noodle Soup

Serves 4

3 CUPS CHICKEN BROTH, FAT REMOVED
2 CUPS WATER
1 TEASPOON DRIED THYME
¼ TEASPOON PEPPER
4 LARGE CHICKEN THIGHS (ABOUT 1¼ POUNDS)
2 MEDIUM CARROTS, THINLY SLICED
1 CUP EGG NOODLES
2 CUPS PACKED FRESH SPINACH LEAVES, TORN INTO BITE-SIZE PIECES
1 CUP FROZEN OR CANNED, DRAINED, WHOLE-KERNEL CORN

1 In large covered saucepan, bring the chicken broth, water, thyme and pepper to a boil over high heat. Add the chicken thighs; return to a boil. Reduce the heat to medium-low; cover and simmer 10 minutes.

2 Transfer chicken thighs to a plate. Return the broth to a boil over medium-high heat. Add the carrots and noodles; cook until the noodles are al dente, about 4 to 6 minutes.

3 Meanwhile, skin the chicken thighs, remove the meat from the bone and cut the meat into bite-size pieces (it will still be slightly pink).

4 Return the chicken to the soup. Add the spinach and corn, and cook at a simmer until chicken is cooked through, about 3 minutes.

PREPARATION TIP
To eliminate having to remove the skin and bones, use already skinned and boned chicken or precut chicken strips used for stir-fries.

Calories: 213 · Protein: 22 g
Fat: 5g/ 21% Calories from Fat ·Carbohydrate: 21 g
Cholesterol: 76 mg · Sodium: 853 mg

Summer Turkey Salad

Serves 4

½ CUP LOW-SODIUM TOMATO-VEGETABLE JUICE
2 TABLESPOONS BALSAMIC VINEGAR
2 TABLESPOONS OLIVE OIL, PREFERABLY EXTRA-VIRGIN
1 TABLESPOON NO-SALT-ADDED TOMATO PASTE
½ TEASPOON DRIED OREGANO
½ TEASPOON SALT
¼ TEASPOON PEPPER
¾ POUND COOKED TURKEY BREAST, CUT INTO 2-INCH BY ½-INCH STRIPS
4 OUNCES ELBOW MACARONI, COOKED
2 CUPS CANNED OR THAWED FROZEN WHOLE-KERNEL CORN
1 TOMATO, CUT INTO ½-INCH CUBES
4 GREEN ONIONS, THINLY SLICED
⅓ CUP CHOPPED FRESH PARSLEY

1 In large serving bowl, combine tomato-vegetable juice, vinegar, oil, tomato paste, oregano, salt and pepper until well mixed.

2 Add turkey, pasta, corn, tomato, green onions and parsley; toss gently to evenly coat.

PREPARATION TIP
To use turkey cutlets for this recipe, in large skillet bring 2 cups water or broth to a boil. Add 1 pound turkey cutlets. Reduce heat to low; simmer, turning once, until turkey is cooked through, about 3 to 4 minutes.

Calories: 378 · Protein: 33 g
Fat: 9 g/ 21% Calories from Fat · Carbohydrate: 44 g
Cholesterol: 71 mg · Sodium: 354 mg

Herbed Turkey Burgers

Serves 4

1	POUND GROUND TURKEY
1	SMALL ONION, MINCED
2	CLOVES GARLIC, MINCED
¼	CUP PACKED FRESH PARSLEY, FINELY CHOPPED
½	CUP FINE UNSEASONED BREADCRUMBS
2	TABLESPOONS DIJON MUSTARD
2	TEASPOONS WORCESTERSHIRE SAUCE
1	EGG WHITE
1	TEASPOON DRIED OREGANO
¼	TEASPOON PEPPER
1	TEASPOON OLIVE OR OTHER VEGETABLE OIL

1 In medium bowl, combine turkey, onion, garlic, parsley, breadcrumbs, mustard, Worcestershire sauce, egg white, oregano and pepper until well mixed.

2 Divide mixture into 4 equal portions; form into ½-inch-thick patties.

3 In large skillet, heat oil over medium-high heat until hot. Add turkey patties; cook until well browned, about 3 to 5 minutes. Turn; cook until well browned, about 2 to 4 minutes.

PREPARATION TIP
Unseasoned breadcrumbs are easily made by taking stale bread and processing in food processor or blender until of desired consistency. Store any extra, tightly sealed, in freezer until needed. Add seasoning just before using, if desired.

Calories: 267 · Protein: 23 g
Fat: 14 g/ 47% calories from fat · Carbohydrate: 13 g
Cholesterol: 77 mg · Sodium: 466 mg

Chicken Parmesan Sandwiches

Serves 4

¼	CUP FINE UNSEASONED BREADCRUMBS
¼	CUP PLUS 4 TEASPOONS GRATED PARMESAN CHEESE (1 OUNCE)
¾	TEASPOON DRIED OREGANO
¼	TEASPOON PEPPER
4	CHICKEN CUTLETS (ABOUT 1¼ POUNDS)
¼	CUP OLIVE OR OTHER VEGETABLE OIL
4	KAISER OR OTHER HARD ROLLS, CUT IN HALF HORIZONTALLY
¼	CUP MAYONNAISE
4	LETTUCE LEAVES
2	MEDIUM PLUM TOMATOES, SLICED

1 In plastic or paper bag, combine breadcrumbs, ¼ cup Parmesan, oregano and pepper. Add chicken cutlets; toss to evenly coat.

2 In large skillet, heat 3 tablespoons oil over medium-high heat until hot. Add chicken; cook, turning once, until cooked through, about 4 to 6 minutes; add remaining 1 tablespoon oil as needed. Remove chicken and keep warm.

3 While skillet is still hot, place one half of each roll in skillet to absorb some of flavored oil.

4 To serve, spread the other half of each roll with mayonnaise; top with lettuce, chicken cutlet, tomato slices and remaining Parmesan cheese.

PREPARATION TIP
To save calories and cut down on fat, eliminate placing the rolls in flavored oil and use reduced-fat mayonnaise instead.

Calories: 495 · Protein: 42 g
Fat: 19 g/ 34% calories from fat · Carbohydrate: 36 g
Cholesterol: 90 mg · Sodium: 585 mg

Chicken and Tiny Star Pasta Stew

Serves 4

2	TABLESPOONS BUTTER OR MARGARINE
3	TABLESPOONS ALL-PURPOSE FLOUR
3½	CUPS CHICKEN BROTH
¾	TEASPOON DRIED THYME
¼	TEASPOON PEPPER
½	CUP TINY PASTA STARS OR OTHER SMALL PASTA SHAPES
2	LARGE CARROTS, THINLY SLICED
¼	POUND MUSHROOMS, THINLY SLICED
1	POUND SKINLESS, BONELESS CHICKEN BREASTS, CUT INTO BITE-SIZE PIECES
10	CHERRY TOMATOES
6	TO 8 GREEN ONIONS, CHOPPED

1 In large saucepan, melt the butter over medium heat. Stir in the flour and cook, stirring, until the flour has completely absorbed the butter, about 1 minute.

2 Increase heat to medium-high; slowly add a small amount of chicken broth; stir until well combined. Gradually add remaining chicken broth, thyme and pepper; bring to a boil, stirring occasionally, until slightly thickened.

3 Add the pasta and carrots and cook, uncovered, about 3 minutes.

4 Add the mushrooms, chicken and whole tomatoes. Return the mixture to a boil over medium-high heat, breaking up the tomatoes with a spoon.

5 Reduce the heat to medium-low; cover and simmer until the chicken is cooked through, about 5 minutes. Stir in green onions.

Calories: 320 · Protein: 32 g
Fat: 8 g/ 22% Calories from Fat · Carbohydrate: 28 g
Cholesterol: 81 mg · Sodium: 649 mg

Orange-Apricot Chicken Wings

Serves 4

½	CUP ORANGE JUICE
¼	CUP APRICOT JAM
3	GREEN ONIONS, COARSELY CHOPPED
2	TABLESPOONS HONEY
1	TABLESPOON DIJON MUSTARD
2	TEASPOONS GRATED ORANGE PEEL (OPTIONAL)
2	CLOVES GARLIC, MINCED
¼	TEASPOON PEPPER
12	CHICKEN WINGS

1 Preheat broiler. Line broiler pan with foil.

2 In large bowl, combine orange juice, apricot jam, green onions, honey, mustard, orange peel, if desired, garlic and pepper. Add chicken wings; toss to evenly coat. Let stand 15 minutes or refrigerate, covered, overnight.

3 Place chicken wings, wing tips up, on prepared pan. Broil 4 inches from heat source until browned, about 8 to 10 minutes. Turn, brush with remaining marinade; cook until browned and cooked through, about 8 to 10 minutes.

PREPARATION TIP
In a microwave-safe bowl, warm the jam in the microwave on High (100% power) for 30 to 60 seconds to easily whisk with the other marinade ingredients.

Calories: 314· Protein: 24 g
Fat: 12 g/ 34% Calories from Fat · Carbohydrate: 27 g
Cholesterol: 70 mg · Sodium: 132 mg

Moroccan-Spiced Chicken Salad

This salad includes all the favorite spices Moroccans enjoy—paprika, ginger, cumin, and coriander, as well as cinnamon.

Serves 4

1	TEASPOON PAPRIKA
¾	TEASPOON SALT
2	SKINLESS, BONELESS CHICKEN BREAST HALVES (ABOUT ¾ POUND)
1	CUP COUSCOUS
2½	CUPS BOILING WATER
2	CUPS COLD WATER
¾	TEASPOON GROUND GINGER
½	TEASPOON CUMIN
½	TEASPOON GROUND CORIANDER
¼	TEASPOON CINNAMON
3	CARROTS, HALVED LENGTHWISE AND THINLY SLICED
2	GREEN PEPPERS, CUT INTO 1-INCH PIECES
1	LARGE TOMATO, FINELY CHOPPED
4	TEASPOONS OLIVE OR OTHER VEGETABLE OIL
1	TABLESPOON HONEY
¼	TEASPOON PEPPER
⅓	CUP CHOPPED FRESH CILANTRO OR PARSLEY

1 Preheat broiler. Combine ½ teaspoon paprika and ¼ teaspoon salt; rub over chicken. Place chicken on broiler pan. Broil 6 inches from heat source until lightly browned, about 4 to 6 minutes. Turn and broil until cooked through, about 4 to 6 minutes. Remove and cool slightly; cut into 1-inch cubes. Set aside.

2 In medium bowl, combine couscous and boiling water. Cover and let stand until couscous has softened and water is absorbed, about 5 to 10 minutes.

3 Meanwhile, in large skillet, combine water, ginger, cumin, coriander and cinnamon. Bring to a boil over medium heat. Add carrots; cook until crisp-tender, about 4 minutes. Add green peppers; cook until crisp-tender, about 1 minute. Transfer carrots and green peppers to large bowl; reserve ¼ cup cooking liquid.

4 To cooked carrots and peppers add remaining ½ teaspoon paprika and ½ teaspoon salt, tomato, oil, honey, pepper and reserved cooking liquid; toss gently to evenly coat.

5 Add chicken, couscous and cilantro; toss gently to evenly coat.

PREPARATION TIP
To get a better salad, after the couscous has softened and absorbed the water, fluff with a fork to separate the grains without crushing them and gently toss with remaining ingredients.

Calories: 368 · Protein: 27 g
Fat: 6 g/ 15% Calories from Fat · Carbohydrate: 50 g
Cholesterol: 49 mg · Sodium: 497 mg

Turkey-Soba Soup

Serves 4

4 CUPS CHICKEN BROTH, FAT REMOVED
2 CUPS WATER
3 MEDIUM CARROTS,
CUT INTO MATCHSTICK PIECES
1 MEDIUM RED ONION, CUT INTO THIN WEDGES
3 SLICES ¼-INCH-THICK FRESH GINGER, MINCED
½ POUND SOBA NOODLES
½ POUND FRESH SPINACH, WASHED,
TRIMMED AND TORN INTO PIECES
¼ CUP CHOPPED CILANTRO (OPTIONAL)
2 TEASPOONS ORIENTAL SESAME OIL
¼ TEASPOON PEPPER
½ POUND COOKED SLICED TURKEY,
CUT INTO ½-INCH-WIDE STRIPS
2 TEASPOONS SESAME SEEDS,
TOASTED, IF DESIRED

1 In large saucepan or Dutch oven, combine broth and water over medium-high heat; bring to a boil. Add carrots, onion and ginger. Reduce heat to low; cover and simmer 5 minutes.

2 Uncover; bring back to a boil. Add noodles; cook until al dente, about 5 to 8 minutes.

3 A minute before noodles are done, add spinach, cilantro, if desired, sesame oil and pepper. Cook until noodles are done and spinach is wilted.

4 Serve broth, noodles and vegetables topped with turkey and sesame seeds.

PREPARATION TIP
If soba noodles can't be found in the international food section of your local supermarket, then substitute linguine or whole-wheat spaghetti, adjusting the cooking time according to package directions.

Calories: 385 · Protein: 30 g
Fat: 8 g/ 18% Calories from Fat · Carbohydrate: 53 g
Cholesterol: 44 mg · Sodium: 1,536 mg

Devilish Drumsticks with Cheese Sauce

Serves 4

1 PACKAGE (3 OUNCES) CREAM CHEESE,
AT ROOM TEMPERATURE
¼ CUP PLAIN YOGURT
2 TABLESPOONS CHOPPED PARSLEY (OPTIONAL)
1 CLOVE GARLIC, MINCED
½ TEASPOON DRIED OREGANO
¼ TEASPOON SALT
¼ TEASPOON PEPPER
3 TABLESPOONS BUTTER OR MARGARINE, MELTED
3 TABLESPOONS HOT PEPPER SAUCE
8 CHICKEN DRUMSTICKS (ABOUT 1¾ POUNDS)

1 Preheat broiler. Line a broiler pan with foil and set aside.

2 In small bowl, beat cream cheese, yogurt, parsley, if desired, garlic, oregano, salt and pepper until well mixed. Cover and refrigerate until serving time.

3 In shallow bowl, combine butter and hot pepper sauce. Dip each drumstick into butter mixture to completely coat; place on prepared pan. Broil 4 inches from heat source until skin is golden, about 7 minutes. Turn; cook until skin is golden, about 7 to 10 minutes.

4 Serve cooked drumsticks with cream cheese-yogurt sauce.

PREPARATION TIP
Everything can be made ahead and served cold or at room temperature. The sauce can be made up to 3 days in advance.

Calories: 339 · Protein: 26 g
Fat: 25 g/ 66% calories from fat · Carbohydrate: 2 g
Cholesterol: 123 mg · Sodium: 605 mg

French Potato Salad

Serves 6

1	POUND BOILING POTATOES, UNPEELED, CUT INTO ½-INCH CHUNKS
8	OUNCES FRESH GREEN BEANS, CUT INTO 2-INCH PIECES
2	SKINLESS, BONELESS CHICKEN BREAST HALVES (ABOUT ¾ POUND), CUT INTO BITE-SIZE PIECES
¼	CUP OLIVE OR OTHER VEGETABLE OIL
2	TABLESPOONS WHITE WINE OR CIDER VINEGAR
1	TABLESPOON DIJON MUSTARD
¾	TEASPOON WORCESTERSHIRE SAUCE
2	TABLESPOONS MINCED FRESH OR 2 TEASPOONS DRIED DILL
¼	TEASPOON SALT
	PEPPER TO TASTE

1 In steamer basket over boiling water, place potatoes over medium heat. Reduce heat to medium-low and steam 10 minutes. Add beans; cover and cook until potatoes are tender and beans are crisp-tender, about 5 to 8 minutes. Transfer to serving bowl; set aside.

2 Place chicken in steamer basket; cover and cook until opaque and cooked through, about 6 to 8 minutes. Transfer to serving bowl with vegetables.

3 To make dressing, in small bowl, combine oil, vinegar, mustard, Worcestershire sauce, dill, salt and pepper.

4 Add dressing to chicken-vegetable mixture; toss gently to evenly coat. Serve warm or at room temperature.

PREPARATION TIP
To save preparation time, substitute 1 package (10 ounces) frozen cut green beans for fresh. Thaw the beans, then run under hot water; cooking isn't necessary. Drain well before adding to the salad.

Calories: 199 · Protein: 11 g
Fat: 10 g/ 45% Calories from Fat · Carbohydrate: 17 g
Cholesterol: 22 mg · Sodium: 205 mg

Hot-and-Sour Chicken Soup

Serves 4

3	CUPS CHICKEN BROTH, FAT REMOVED
½	CUP WATER
4	OUNCES SMALL MUSHROOMS
½	CUP CANNED SLICED BAMBOO SHOOTS
3	SLICES ¼-INCH-THICK FRESH GINGER
2	CLOVES GARLIC, MINCED
2	TEASPOONS REDUCED-SODIUM SOY SAUCE
½	TEASPOON RED PEPPER FLAKES
2	SKINLESS, BONELESS CHICKEN BREAST HALVES (ABOUT ¾ POUND), CUT ACROSS GRAIN INTO ¼-INCH SLICES
1	TABLESPOON ORIENTAL SESAME OIL
3	TABLESPOONS RED WINE OR CIDER VINEGAR
2	TABLESPOONS CORNSTARCH
1	EGG, BEATEN
2	GREEN ONIONS, FINELY CHOPPED
¼	CUP CILANTRO (OPTIONAL)

1 In medium saucepan, combine broth, water, mushrooms, bamboo shoots, ginger, garlic, soy sauce and red pepper flakes over medium-high heat. Bring to a boil. Reduce heat to low; cover and simmer 5 minutes.

2 In small bowl, combine chicken and sesame oil; toss to evenly coat. In another small bowl, combine vinegar and cornstarch until well mixed.

3 Increase heat to medium-high; bring to a boil. Add chicken. Stirring constantly, slowly pour in egg. Stir in vinegar-cornstarch mixture. Cook, stirring occasionally, until chicken is cooked through and soup slightly thickened, about 3 minutes.

4 Stir in green onions. Remove ginger slices. Serve sprinkled with cilantro, if desired.

Calories: 228 · Protein: 31 g
Fat: 7 g/ 27% Calories from Fat · Carbohydrate: 8 g
Cholesterol: 119 mg · Sodium: 933 mg

Chicken Breasts with Apricots and Almonds

The mild curry flavor of this delicious dish captures the flavors of an Indian biryani,
which generally includes meat or poultry, spices, dried fruit and nuts.

Serves 4

3	TABLESPOONS ALL-PURPOSE FLOUR
2	TEASPOONS CURRY POWDER
½	TEASPOON SALT
¼	TEASPOON PEPPER
4	SKINLESS, BONELESS CHICKEN BREAST HALVES (ABOUT 1¼ POUNDS)
1	TABLESPOON BUTTER OR MARGARINE
1	TABLESPOON OLIVE OR OTHER VEGETABLE OIL
1	CUP CHICKEN BROTH, FAT REMOVED
2	TABLESPOONS TOMATO PASTE
½	CUP GOLDEN OR DARK SEEDLESS RAISINS
½	TEASPOON SUGAR
½	CUP DRIED APRICOTS, COARSELY CHOPPED
2	GREEN ONIONS, COARSELY CHOPPED
¼	CUP SLICED ALMONDS, TOASTED

1 In plastic or paper bag, combine flour, 1 teaspoon curry powder, salt and pepper until well mixed. Add chicken; toss to evenly coat. Remove chicken and reserve excess seasoned flour.

2 In large skillet, heat butter and oil over medium-high heat until butter melts. Add coated chicken; cook, turning occasionally, until brown, about 8 to 10 minutes. Remove and keep warm.

3 Reduce heat to medium. Add 1 tablespoon reserved seasoned flour to skillet; cook, stirring, until flour is incorporated, about 1 minute.

4 Stir in remaining 1 teaspoon curry powder, broth, tomato paste, raisins and sugar. Increase heat to medium-high. Bring to a boil.

5 Add apricots and chicken. Reduce heat to medium-low; cover and simmer until chicken is cooked through, about 5 minutes. Stir in green onions.

6 Serve chicken topped with sauce and sprinkled with almonds.

PREPARATION TIP
To toast almonds, place in single layer on baking sheet; bake in 375° oven 5 minutes or until lightly browned.

Calories: 411 · Protein: 37 g
Fat: 12 g/ 26% Calories from Fat · Carbohydrate: 41 g
Cholesterol: 90 mg · Sodium: 713 mg

Spicy Chicken-Peanut Stir-Fry

The crunch in this easy Chinese stir-fry comes from both the peanuts and the celery.

Serves 4

4	SKINLESS, BONELESS CHICKEN BREAST HALVES (ABOUT 1¼ POUNDS), CUT INTO BITE-SIZE PIECES
2	TABLESPOONS REDUCED-SODIUM SOY SAUCE
2	TEASPOONS ORIENTAL SESAME OIL
1	TABLESPOON CORNSTARCH
⅔	CUP CHICKEN BROTH, FAT REMOVED
2	DROPS HOT PEPPER SAUCE
2	TABLESPOONS OLIVE OR OTHER VEGETABLE OIL
2	RIBS CELERY, THINLY SLICED
6	LARGE GREEN ONIONS, SLICED DIAGONALLY INTO ½-INCH PIECES
1	LARGE YELLOW OR GREEN PEPPER, CUT INTO BITE-SIZE PIECES
3	SLICES ¼-INCH-THICK FRESH GINGER, CUT INTO SLIVERS
3	CLOVES GARLIC, MINCED
½	CUP UNSALTED PEANUTS
¼	TEASPOON PEPPER

1 In medium bowl, combine chicken, 1 tablespoon soy sauce, sesame oil and 1½ teaspoons cornstarch; toss to evenly coat. Let stand.

2 In 1-cup measure or small bowl, combine remaining 1 tablespoon soy sauce and 1½ teaspoons cornstarch, broth and hot pepper sauce.

3 In large skillet or wok, heat 1 tablespoon olive oil over medium-high heat until hot. Add chicken and marinade; cook, stirring constantly, until chicken is still slightly pink in center, about 3 minutes. Remove and keep warm.

4 To same skillet, add remaining 1 tablespoon olive oil. Add celery, green onions, yellow pepper, ginger and garlic; Cook, stirring constantly, until green onions begin to wilt about 3 minutes.

5 Return chicken to skillet; add peanuts and pepper. Stir broth-cornstarch mixture; add to skillet. Bring to a boil. Cook, stirring constantly until vegetables are crisp-tender and chicken is cooked through, about 3 to 5 minutes.

PREPARATION TIP

To save time and get a head start on dinner, cut the chicken and marinade ahead of time; have the vegetables cut and ready-to-go; and have the broth-cornstarch mixture already combined.

Calories: 375 · Protein: 39 g
Fat: 20 g/ 48% Calories from Fat · Carbohydrate: 10 g
Cholesterol: 82 mg · Sodium: 579 mg

Chicken Vegetable Stir-Fry

To complete the meal just add rice, which, if started just before the stir-fry,
will be ready to serve under the vegetables.

Serves 4

3 TABLESPOONS VEGETABLE OIL

2 TABLESPOONS REDUCED-SODIUM SOY SAUCE

1½ TABLESPOONS CORNSTARCH

2 SKINLESS, BONELESS CHICKEN BREAST HALVES
(ABOUT ¾ POUND), CUT INTO 1-INCH CUBES

¾ CUP CHICKEN BROTH, FAT REMOVED

½ TEASPOON SUGAR

¼ TEASPOON RED PEPPER FLAKES

1 LARGE RED PEPPER,
CUT INTO 1-INCH SQUARES

1 MEDIUM RED ONION, HALVED,
CUT INTO ¼-INCH SLICES

1 LARGE STALK BROCCOLI, CUT INTO FLORETS,
STEM CUT INTO ¼-INCH SLICES

2 CLOVES GARLIC, MINCED

1 CAN (8 OUNCES) SLICED WATER CHESTNUTS,
DRAINED

¼ CUP WALNUT HALVES OR PIECES

1 In medium bowl, combine 1 tablespoon each oil, soy sauce and cornstarch until well mixed. Add chicken; toss until evenly coated.

2 In small bowl or container, combine remaining 1 tablespoon soy sauce, 1½ teaspoons cornstarch, broth, sugar and red pepper flakes; set aside.

3 In large skillet or wok, heat 1 tablespoon oil over medium-high heat until hot. Add chicken and marinade; cook, stirring constantly, until chicken is still slightly pink in center, about 3 minutes. Remove and keep warm.

4 Add remaining 1 tablespoon oil to skillet. Add red pepper, onion, broccoli, garlic and water chestnuts; cook, stirring constantly, until onion begins to wilt, about 2 to 3 minutes.

5 Return chicken to skillet with walnuts. Stir reserved broth-cornstarch mixture; add to chicken-vegetable mixture. Bring to a boil.

6 Cook, stirring constantly, until chicken is cooked through and vegetables are crisp-tender, about 2 to 3 minutes.

PREPARATION TIP
To reduce the amount of sodium in this dish use "lite" soy sauce or take ordinary soy sauce and dilute it by ⅓ with water or reduced-sodium chicken broth.

Calories: 295 · Protein: 22 g
Fat: 16 g/ 48% Calories from Fat · Carbohydrate: 18 g
Cholesterol: 44 mg · Sodium: 555 mg

Lime Grilled Turkey Sandwiches

Serves 4

¼	CUP LIME JUICE
1	TABLESPOON OLIVE OR OTHER VEGETABLE OIL
½	TEASPOON SALT
¼	TEASPOON PEPPER
1	POUND TURKEY CUTLETS, POUNDED ¼ INCH THICK
⅓	CUP MAYONNAISE
2	TABLESPOONS CHOPPED CILANTRO (OPTIONAL)
1	TEASPOON GRATED LIME PEEL (OPTIONAL)
1	SMALL AVOCADO, PEELED AND SLICED
4	CLUB OR OTHER HARD ROLLS, CUT IN HALF LENGTHWISE
4	LETTUCE LEAVES
¼	CUP CRANBERRY SAUCE

1 Prepare broiler or grill according to manufacturer's directions. In shallow bowl, combine 2 tablespoons lime juice, oil, salt and pepper until well mixed. Add cutlets; toss to evenly coat.

2 Broil or grill 4 inches from heat source, turning once, until cooked through, about 6 minutes. Meanwhile, in small bowl, combine 1 tablespoon lime juice, mayonnaise, cilantro and lime peel, if desired; set aside.

3 Toss avocado with remaining lime juice. Broil or grill rolls until lightly toasted, about 30 seconds.

4 To serve, spread both sides of rolls with lime mayonnaise; layer ¼ each lettuce, chicken cutlet, avocado slices and 1 tablespoon cranberry sauce.

Lemon Turkey Scallops

Serves 4

3	TABLESPOONS ALL-PURPOSE FLOUR
2	CLOVES GARLIC, MINCED
¼	CUP CHOPPED PARSLEY (OPTIONAL)
½	TEASPOON SALT
¼	TEASPOON PEPPER
8	SMALL TURKEY SCALLOPS (ABOUT 1½ POUNDS)
4	TABLESPOONS BUTTER OR MARGARINE
2	TABLESPOONS OLIVE OR OTHER VEGETABLE OIL
2	LEMONS, ONE THINLY SLICED, ONE JUICED

1 In plastic or paper bag, combine flour, garlic, parsley, salt and pepper until well combined. Add turkey; toss to evenly coat.

2 In large skillet, heat 1 tablespoon each butter and oil over medium-high heat until butter is melted. Add turkey scallops in single layer; cook, turning once, until golden brown, about 6 minutes. Remove and keep warm. Repeat with remaining turkey scallops; add another 1 tablespoon each butter and oil as needed. Remove and keep warm.

3 In same skillet, add remaining 2 tablespoons butter and lemon juice. Increase heat to high; cook, stirring, 1 minute.

4 Add lemon slices to skillet; cook 30 seconds. To serve, arrange lemon slices over turkey scallops and top with lemon sauce.

PREPARATION TIP
Thinly sliced turkey cutlets are now appearing in most supermarkets. Use this versatile cut in almost any recipe that calls for veal cutlets or chicken breasts.

Calories: 870 · Protein: 38 g
Fat: 43 g/ 45% Calories from Fat · Carbohydrate: 84 g
Cholesterol: 75 mg · Sodium: 1,170 mg

Calories: 379 · Protein: 41 g
Fat: 21 g/ 49% Calories from Fat · Carbohydrate: 7 g
Cholesterol: 137 mg · Sodium: 417 mg

Honey-Thyme Turkey with Lemon Noodles

Serves 4

2	TABLESPOONS PLUS 1 TEASPOON BUTTER OR MARGARINE
2	TABLESPOONS HONEY
1	TEASPOON DRIED THYME
¾	TEASPOON SALT
½	TEASPOON PEPPER
¾	POUND WIDE EGG NOODLES
4	TURKEY CUTLETS (ABOUT 1 POUND)
3	TABLESPOONS LEMON JUICE
1½	TEASPOONS GRATED LEMON PEEL (OPTIONAL)

1 Preheat broiler. Line broiler pan with foil and lightly grease. Bring large pot of water to a boil over high heat.

2 In small skillet or saucepan, combine 2 tablespoons butter, honey, thyme and ¼ teaspoon each salt and pepper over low heat; cook until butter is melted, about 6 minutes.

3 Add noodles to boiling water; cook until tender, about 8 to 10 minutes.

4 Place turkey cutlets on broiler pan. Brush with half honey-butter mixture; broil 4 inches from heat source until lightly browned, about 4 minutes. Turn; brush with remaining honey-butter mixture; broil until cooked through, about 3 to 5 minutes.

5 Drain noodles; add remaining 1 teaspoon butter, ½ teaspoon salt, ¼ teaspoon pepper, lemon juice, lemon peel, if desired, and any juices from broiler pan; toss to evenly coat. Serve turkey with noodles.

Chicken Breasts with Pineapple-Pepper Relish

Serves 4

1	CAN (16 OUNCES) CRUSHED PINEAPPLE IN JUICE, DRAINED
1	RED PEPPER, DICED
1	GREEN ONION, FINELY CHOPPED
¼	CUP PLUS 2 TABLESPOONS CHILI SAUCE
¼	CUP PLUS 1 TABLESPOON THAWED PINEAPPLE JUICE CONCENTRATE
2	TABLESPOONS HONEY
2	TEASPOONS RED WINE VINEGAR
¼	TEASPOON RED PEPPER FLAKES
4	SKINLESS, BONELESS CHICKEN BREAST HALVES (ABOUT 1¼ POUNDS)

1 Preheat broiler. Line broiler pan with foil.

2 To make relish, in medium bowl, combine pineapple, red pepper, green onion, 2 tablespoons chili sauce, 1 tablespoon pineapple juice concentrate, 1 tablespoon honey, vinegar and pepper flakes until well combined. Let stand.

3 In small bowl, combine remaining ¼ cup chili sauce, remaining ¼ cup pineapple juice concentrate and remaining 1 tablespoon honey until well combined.

4 Place chicken on broiler pan; brush with half chili-pineapple mixture. Broil 4 inches from heat source until lightly browned, about 4 minutes. Turn; brush with remaining chili-pineapple mixture. Broil until chicken is cooked through, about 4 to 6 minutes.

5 Serve chicken with relish.

Calories: 552 · Protein: 39 g
Fat: 12 g/19% Calories from Fat · Carbohydrate: 71 g
Cholesterol: 169 mg · Sodium: 578 mg

Calories: 299 · Protein: 28 g
Fat: 2 g/ 6% Calories from Fat · Carbohydrate: 44 g
Cholesterol: 66 mg · Sodium: 419 mg

Minted Chicken Salad

Serves 4

1	POUND SMALL RED POTATOES, HALVED
8	OUNCES FRESH GREEN BEANS, CUT INTO 2-INCH PIECES
1	CUP REDUCED-SODIUM CHICKEN BROTH, FAT REMOVED
2	SKINLESS, BONELESS CHICKEN BREAST HALVES (ABOUT ¾ POUND)
¾	CUP BUTTERMILK
2	TABLESPOONS FRESH LEMON JUICE
1	TABLESPOON HONEY
¼	TEASPOON SALT
¼	TEASPOON CAYENNE PEPPER
⅓	CUP CHOPPED FRESH MINT
12	OUNCES PACKED FRESH SPINACH LEAVES, WASHED AND TORN (8 CUPS)
2	CUPS CHERRY TOMATOES, HALVED
1	CUP CRUMBLED FETA CHEESE (ABOUT 3 OUNCES)

1 In medium saucepan, place potatoes and enough water to cover over high heat. Bring to a boil; cook, partially covered, just until barely tender, about 10 to 15 minutes. Add green beans during last 2 minutes. Drain.

2 Meanwhile, in medium skillet, combine broth and chicken over medium heat. Bring to a boil. Reduce heat to low; simmer, uncovered, until chicken is cooked through, about 5 to 8 minutes. Remove chicken (reserve broth for another use) and cool slightly; cut across the grain into ½-inch-thick slices. Set aside.

3 To make dressing, in large bowl, combine buttermilk, lemon juice, honey, salt and cayenne until well mixed. Add mint; stir until well mixed. Add reserved potatoes, reserved green beans, reserved chicken, spinach and tomatoes; toss gently to evenly coat.

4 Top with feta cheese.

Calories: 362 · Protein: 35 g
Fat: 8 g/19% Calories from Fat · Carbohydrate: 43 g
Cholesterol: 71 mg · Sodium: 680 mg

Chicken Noodle Salad

Everything here is generally found in the best chicken noodle soups—
tender chicken, noodles, carrots, and peas.

Serves 4

1½	CUPS REDUCED-SODIUM CHICKEN BROTH, FAT REMOVED
¼	TEASPOON PEPPER
¼	TEASPOON GROUND GINGER
2	SMALL SKINLESS, BONELESS CHICKEN BREAST HALVES (ABOUT ¾ POUND)
2	CARROTS, HALVED LENGTHWISE, THINLY SLICED
1	CUP FROZEN PEAS
⅓	CUP REDUCED-FAT SOUR CREAM
⅓	CUP CHOPPED FRESH DILL
2	TABLESPOONS REDUCED-FAT MAYONNAISE
1	TABLESPOON LEMON JUICE
½	TEASPOON GRATED LEMON PEEL
½	TEASPOON SALT
8	OUNCES FETTUCCINE, COOKED, DRAINED
2	RIBS CELERY, HALVED LENGTHWISE, THINLY SLICED

1 In large skillet, combine broth, pepper and ginger over medium heat. Bring to a boil. Reduce heat to low. Add chicken; cover and simmer until chicken is cooked through, about 10 minutes. Add carrots during last 2 minutes of cooking. Add peas; remove from heat.

2 Drain chicken and vegetables, reserving broth. When chicken is cool enough to handle, cut into ½-inch cubes.

3 In large bowl, combine ½ cup reserved broth, sour cream, dill, mayonnaise, lemon juice, lemon peel and salt.

4 Add reserved chicken and vegetables, fettuccine and celery; toss gently to evenly coat.

PREPARATION TIP

To make this salad even faster and easier, buy cooked chicken or turkey at the deli counter to eliminate having to cook the chicken. This is also a great way to use leftover cooked chicken.

Calories: 415 · Protein: 32 g
Fat: 8 g/ 17% Calories from Fat · Carbohydrate: 54 g
Cholesterol: 110 mg · Sodium: 554 mg

California Chicken Salad with Avocado

Serves 4

1¼	POUNDS SMALL RED POTATOES, QUARTERED
1	CUP REDUCED-SODIUM CHICKEN BROTH, FAT REMOVED
¼	TEASPOON DRIED ROSEMARY, CRUMBLED
2	SMALL SKINLESS, BONELESS CHICKEN BREAST HALVES (ABOUT ¾ POUND)
2	BUNCHES WATERCRESS, TOUGH STEMS REMOVED
4	TOMATOES, 2 CUT INTO 6 WEDGES, 2 FINELY CHOPPED
¼	CUP LIME JUICE
1	TABLESPOON OLIVE OIL, PREFERABLY EXTRA-VIRGIN
½	TEASPOON SALT
⅓	CUP DICED AVOCADO

1 In medium saucepan, combine potatoes and enough water to cover over medium-high heat; cook until potatoes are firm, about 10 minutes. Drain and set aside.

2 In large skillet, combine broth and rosemary over medium heat; bring to a boil. Add chicken. Reduce heat to low; cover and simmer, turning once, until chicken is cooked through, about 10 minutes. Remove chicken; reserve chicken broth for another use. When cool enough to handle, cut diagonally into ½-inch slices.

3 In large bowl, combine potatoes, watercress and tomato wedges. To make dressing, in small bowl, combine finely chopped tomatoes, lime juice, oil and salt until well mixed. Reserve ¼ cup dressing. Add remaining dressing and chicken to potato mixture; toss gently to evenly coat. Serve drizzled with remaining dressing and topped with avocado.

Calories: 283 · Protein: 23 g
Fat: 7 g/ 22% Calories from Fat · Carbohydrate: 35 g
Cholesterol: 41 mg · Sodium: 413 mg

Spaghetti Primavera with Chicken

Serves 4

5	TABLESPOONS LIGHT OLIVE OR OTHER VEGETABLE OIL
2	SMALL CHICKEN BREAST HALVES (ABOUT ¾ POUND), CUT INTO 1-INCH CUBES
½	POUND MUSHROOMS, CUT INTO ¼-INCH-THICK SLICES
1	MEDIUM YELLOW OR GREEN PEPPER, CUT INTO SLIVERS
6	TO 8 GREEN ONIONS, COARSELY CHOPPED
2	CLOVES GARLIC, MINCED
8	OUNCES SPAGHETTI, COOKED
¼	CUP CHOPPED FRESH OR 1 TEASPOON DRIED DILL
¾	TEASPOON SALT
¼	TEASPOON PEPPER

1 In large skillet or flameproof casserole, heat 2 tablespoons oil over medium-high heat until hot. Add chicken; cook, stirring occasionally, until it turns white, about 2 to 3 minutes.

2 Add remaining 3 tablespoons oil, mushrooms, yellow pepper, green onions and garlic; cook, stirring occasionally, until vegetables are softened, about 2 to 3 minutes.

3 Stir in cooked spaghetti, dill, salt and pepper; toss gently until well combined.

PREPARATION TIP
If desired, other thinly sliced or small, whole vegetables can be substituted. Try French-cut green beans, zucchini, yellow summer squash, red onion or peas.

Calories: 481 · Protein: 29 g
Fat: 19 g/ 35% Calories from Fat · Carbohydrate: 48 g
Cholesterol: 49 mg · Sodium: 473 mg

Orange Chicken and Oriental Noodles

Prepackaged ramen noodles, which cook in minutes,
form the basis for this tasty Chinese-style dinner.

Serves 6

1	TABLESPOON CORNSTARCH
¼	TEASPOON PEPPER
2	SMALL SKINLESS, BONELESS CHICKEN BREAST HALVES (ABOUT ¾ POUND), CUT ACROSS THE GRAIN INTO ¼-INCH-THICK STRIPS
1	TABLESPOON ORIENTAL SESAME OIL
6	CUPS WATER
2	PACKAGES (3½ OUNCES EACH) INSTANT CHICKEN-FLAVOR RAMEN NOODLES
2	TABLESPOONS VEGETABLE OIL
3	CUPS SHREDDED CABBAGE (ABOUT 8 OUNCES)
4	SLICES ¼-INCH-THICK FRESH GINGER, MINCED
3	CLOVES GARLIC, MINCED
1	CAN (8 OUNCES) SLICED WATER CHESTNUTS, DRAINED
4	GREEN ONIONS, CUT INTO 1-INCH PIECES
1	CAN (11 OUNCES) MANDARIN ORANGES, DRAINED
3	TABLESPOONS REDUCED-SODIUM SOY SAUCE

1 In plastic or paper bag, combine cornstarch and pepper. Add chicken; shake to lightly coat. Transfer chicken to bowl; add sesame oil and toss to evenly coat.

2 In large saucepan or Dutch oven, combine water and seasoning packets from noodles over high heat; bring to a boil.

3 Meanwhile, in large skillet, heat 1 table-spoon oil over medium-high heat until hot. Add coated chicken; cook, stirring, until chicken loses its pink color, about 3 to 4 minutes. Remove and keep warm.

4 To same skillet, add remaining 1 table-spoon oil, cabbage, ginger, garlic and water chestnuts; cook, stirring, until cabbage is wilted, about 3 minutes.

5 Add ramen noodles to boiling water; cook until al dente, about 3 minutes. Drain well.

6 Return chicken to skillet; add green onions, reserved noodles, mandarin oranges and soy sauce. Toss to evenly combine.

PREPARATION TIP

For stronger, more pronounced chicken flavor, cook noodles in lightly salted water and add one seasoning packet to noodles in Step 6.

Calories: 362 · Protein: 23 g
Fat: 14 g/ 32% Calories from Fat · Carbohydrate: 37 g
Cholesterol: 44 mg · Sodium: 568 mg

MEAT DISHES

Spring Lamb and Asparagus Salad

*A springtime treat of hearty sweet potatoes, tart arugula, tender lamb
and crisp-tender asparagus.*

Serves 4

1¼ POUNDS SWEET POTATOES, PEELED,
    CUT INTO ½-INCH CUBES

1   POUND ASPARAGUS, TRIMMED,
    CUT INTO 2-INCH PIECES

¼   CUP FROZEN APPLE JUICE CONCENTRATE,
    THAWED

¼   CUP REDUCED-SODIUM CHICKEN BROTH,
    FAT REMOVED

1   TABLESPOON RICE WINE VINEGAR

1   TABLESPOON DIJON MUSTARD

2   TEASPOONS OLIVE OR OTHER VEGETABLE OIL

½   TEASPOON GROUND GINGER

¾   TEASPOON SALT

1   RED PEPPER, CUT INTO 1-INCH PIECES

1   YELLOW PEPPER, CUT INTO 1-INCH PIECES

¾   POUND WELL-TRIMMED BONELESS
    LAMB SHOULDER

4   CUPS ARUGULA, TOUGH STEMS REMOVED

1 Preheat broiler. In large pot, combine sweet potatoes and enough water to cover over medium-high heat; cook until sweet potatoes are almost tender, about 8 minutes. Add asparagus; cook until asparagus is crisp-tender and sweet potatoes are tender, about 2 minutes. Drain well.

2 In large bowl, combine apple juice concentrate, broth, vinegar, mustard, oil, ginger and ½ teaspoon salt. Add sweet potatoes, asparagus and raw peppers; toss gently to evenly coat.

3 Place lamb on broiler pan; sprinkle with remaining ¼ teaspoon salt. Broil 6 inches from heat source, turning once, until medium, about 8 to 10 minutes. Let stand 10 minutes. Cut into 1-inch by ¼-inch strips; reserve any juices.

4 Add lamb strips and arugula to vegetable mixture; toss gently to evenly coat.

PREPARATION TIP
If desired, watercress, chicory or escarole can be substituted for arugula.

Calories: 331 · Protein: 22 g
Fat: 10 g/ 27% Calories from Fat · Carbohydrate: 38 g
Cholesterol: 58 mg · Sodium: 627 mg

Shells with Pork Tenderloin and Eggplant

Serves 4

1	TABLESPOON ALL-PURPOSE FLOUR
8	OUNCES PORK TENDERLOIN, CUT INTO ½-INCH CHUNKS
2	TABLESPOONS OLIVE OR OTHER VEGETABLE OIL
1	TABLESPOON MILD CHILI POWDER
8	OUNCES EGGPLANT, PEELED, CUT INTO ½-INCH CHUNKS (ABOUT 2½ CUPS)
3	CLOVES GARLIC, MINCED
¾	TEASPOON GROUND GINGER
¾	TEASPOON SALT
¼	TEASPOON GROUND ALLSPICE
¼	TEASPOON PEPPER
2	CUPS CHERRY TOMATOES, HALVED
1	CUP COOKED RED KIDNEY BEANS, RINSED
3	TABLESPOONS CHOPPED FRESH PARSLEY
2	TABLESPOONS BALSAMIC VINEGAR
10	OUNCES PASTA SHELLS, COOKED, HOT

1 In plastic or paper bag, place flour. Add pork; toss to evenly coat. In large nonstick skillet, heat 1 tablespoon oil over medium heat until hot.

2 Stir in chili powder; cook, stirring constantly, until fragrant, about 30 seconds. Add pork; cook, stirring frequently, until lightly browned, about 1 minute. Remove pork and keep warm.

3 To same skillet add remaining 1 tablespoon oil, eggplant, garlic, ginger, salt, allspice and pepper; cook, stirring, about 3 minutes.

4 Add 1 cup water. Increase heat to medium-high; cook, stirring frequently, until eggplant is almost tender, about 3 minutes.

5 Add reserved pork, tomatoes and beans; cook until pork is cooked through, about 4 minutes. Stir in parsley and vinegar.

6 Serve pasta with pork-eggplant mixture.

Calories: 492 · Protein: 26 g
Fat: 12 g/ 21% Calories from Fat · Carbohydrate: 70 g
Cholesterol: 37 mg · Sodium: 559 mg

Pork Parmesan

Serves 4

3	TABLESPOONS FINE UNSEASONED BREADCRUMBS
3	TABLESPOONS GRATED PARMESAN CHEESE
1½	TEASPOONS OREGANO
½	TEASPOON PEPPER
1	EGG WHITE
4	MEDIUM ¼-INCH-THICK BONELESS PORK CUTLETS (ABOUT 1¼ POUNDS)
1	TABLESPOON BUTTER OR MARGARINE
2	TABLESPOONS VEGETABLE OIL
1	LEMON, CUT INTO WEDGES

1 In plastic or paper bag or shallow dish, combine breadcrumbs, Parmesan cheese, oregano and pepper. In shallow bowl, beat egg white until frothy.

2 Dip pork into egg white to evenly coat. Add cutlets to seasoned breadcrumbs; toss to evenly coat. Remove cutlets.

3 In large skillet, heat butter and 1 tablespoon oil over medium-high heat until butter is melted. Add coated pork; cook, turning once, until golden brown and cooked through, about 6 to 8 minutes. Add remaining 1 tablespoon oil to prevent sticking.

4 Serve with lemon wedges.

PREPARATION TIP
To make your own pork cutlets, buy a boneless pork loin or, to save money, top loin or rib pork chops and remove the bone for another use; then thinly slice.

Calories: 326 · Protein: 32 g
Fat: 19 g/ 52% Calories from Fat · Carbohydrate: 7 g
Cholesterol: 107 mg · Sodium: 226 mg

Fettuccine Alla Carbonara

This version has only one-fifth the amount of fat compared to the true classic dish without losing the rich, creamy texture and wonderful flavor.

Serves 4

⅔   CUP LOW-FAT (1%) COTTAGE CHEESE
1   TABLESPOON OLIVE OR OTHER VEGETABLE OIL
4   OUNCES CANADIAN BACON, DICED
12   OUNCES FETTUCCINE
1   LARGE ONION, FINELY CHOPPED
3   CLOVES GARLIC, MINCED
½   CUP REDUCED-SODIUM BEEF BROTH, FAT REMOVED
¼   TEASPOON PEPPER
2   TABLESPOONS REDUCED-FAT SOUR CREAM
2   TABLESPOONS GRATED PARMESAN CHEESE
¼   CUP CHOPPED FRESH PARSLEY

PREPARATION TIP

For a complete meal, serve with a red leaf lettuce salad dressed with a light oil and vinegar dressing and a fruit sherbet for dessert.

1 In large pot, bring to a boil enough water to cook pasta over medium-high heat. In food processor or blender, process cottage cheese until smooth, about 1 minute. Set aside.

2 In large nonstick skillet, heat oil over medium heat until hot. Add bacon; cook until lightly crisped, about 5 minutes. Remove bacon and set aside.

3 Place fettuccine in boiling water; cook until al dente, about 8 to 12 minutes.

4 Meanwhile, in same skillet, add onion and garlic; cook, stirring frequently, until onion is softened, about 5 to 7 minutes. Add broth and pepper. Reduce heat to low. Stir in cottage cheese purée until well mixed. Stir in reserved bacon, sour cream and Parmesan until well mixed. Cook 1 minute.

5 Transfer sauce to large serving bowl. Drain fettuccine. Add to cheese-bacon mixture with parsley; toss gently to evenly coat. Serve immediately.

Calories: 478 · Protein: 25 g
Fat: 11 g/ 20% Calories from Fat · Carbohydrate: 69 g
Cholesterol: 101 mg · Sodium: 700 mg

Italian Beef Salad

Serves 4

8	OUNCES PENNE PASTA
1	PACKAGE (10 OUNCES) FROZEN ITALIAN GREEN BEANS, THAWED
4	TEASPOONS OLIVE OR OTHER VEGETABLE OIL
¾	POUND BONELESS BEEF SIRLOIN, CUT INTO 2-INCH BY ¼-INCH STRIPS
1	ONION, FINELY CHOPPED
3	CLOVES GARLIC, MINCED
1	CARROT, HALVED LENGTHWISE AND THINLY SLICED
1½	POUNDS TOMATOES, FINELY CHOPPED
½	CUP CHOPPED FRESH BASIL
2	TABLESPOONS BALSAMIC VINEGAR
½	TEASPOON SALT
2	OUNCES SHAVED PARMESAN CHEESE

1 In large pot, combine boiling water and pasta over high heat; cook until pasta is just tender, about 8 to 10 minutes. Add green beans during last 2 minutes of cooking. Drain well and set aside.

2 In large nonstick skillet, heat oil over medium heat under hot. Add beef; cook, stirring frequently, until no longer pink, about 3 minutes. Remove and keep warm.

3 To same skillet add onion and garlic; cook, stirring frequently, until onion is tender, about 5 minutes. Add carrot; cook, stirring frequently, until carrot is crisp-tender, about 4 minutes. Transfer to large bowl. Add tomatoes, basil, vinegar and salt; toss to evenly coat.

4 Add reserved pasta, beans and beef; toss gently to evenly coat. Serve topped with the shaved Parmesan cheese.

Beef and Broccoli with Mustard Vinaigrette

Serves 4

⅓	CUP RED WINE VINEGAR
⅓	CUP REDUCED-SODIUM CHICKEN BROTH, FAT REMOVED
2	TABLESPOONS DIJON MUSTARD
4	TEASPOONS CAPERS, RINSED AND DRAINED
1	TABLESPOON PLUS 2 TEASPOONS OLIVE OIL
½	TEASPOON DRIED TARRAGON, CRUMBLED
¼	TEASPOON SALT
3	CUPS BROCCOLI FLORETS
1½	POUNDS ALL-PURPOSE POTATOES, CUT INTO ½-INCH CUBES
1	CUP PEELED BABY CARROTS
1	RED PEPPER, CUT INTO ½-INCH PIECES
¾	POUND BONELESS BEEF SIRLOIN

1 Preheat broiler. In large bowl, combine vinegar, broth, 1 tablespoon mustard, capers, oil, tarragon and salt until well mixed; set aside.

2 In large pot, combine boiling water and broccoli over high heat; cook until broccoli is just blanched, about 1 minute. Remove and set aside. Add potatoes and carrots; cook until potatoes are tender, about 7 minutes. Drain. Add potatoes, carrots and red pepper to vinegar mixture; toss gently to evenly coat.

3 Place beef on broiler pan; brush with remaining 1 tablespoon mustard; broil 6 inches from heat source until medium-rare, about 8 to 10 minutes. Let stand 10 minutes. When cool, cut into thin slices on diagonal and then cut into 1-inch pieces; reserve juices. Add reserved broccoli, beef, and reserved meat juices to vegetables; toss gently to evenly coat.

Calories: 521 · Protein: 35 g
Fat: 14 g/ 24% Calories from Fat · Carbohydrate: 65 g
Cholesterol: 63 mg · Sodium: 617 mg

Calories: 342 · Protein: 26 g
Fat: 11 g/ 28% Calories from Fat · Carbohydrate: 34 g
Cholesterol: 57 mg · Sodium: 548 mg

Microwave Baked Potato Stroganoff

Serves 4

4	MEDIUM BAKING POTATOES (ABOUT 2 POUNDS)
2	TABLESPOONS BUTTER OR MARGARINE
1	MEDIUM ONION, COARSELY CHOPPED
4	OUNCES MUSHROOMS, CUT INTO ¼-INCH-THICK SLICES
¾	CUP BEEF BROTH, FAT REMOVED
1	TABLESPOON PAPRIKA (OPTIONAL)
½	TEASPOON SALT
⅛	TEASPOON PEPPER
12	OUNCES COOKED ROAST BEEF, CUT INTO ½-INCH CUBES (ABOUT 3 CUPS)
¾	CUP SOUR CREAM
2	GREEN ONIONS, CHOPPED FOR GARNISH
¼	CUP SHREDDED CHEDDAR CHEESE, FOR GARNISH

1 With sharp knife, cut 1 or 2 vent slits in potatoes. Place end to end in circle in microwave; cook on High (100% power) until tender, about 15 to 20 minutes.

2 In medium skillet, heat butter over medium-high heat until melted. Add onion; cook until golden, about 5 minutes. Add mushrooms; cook until coated, about 1 to 2 minutes.

3 Add beef broth, paprika, if desired, salt and pepper. Reduce heat to medium-low; cover and simmer until mushrooms are just tender, about 2 to 3 minutes. Stir in roast beef and sour cream. Remove skillet from heat.

4 To serve, cut open potatoes, top with roast beef-mushroom mixture. Garnish with green onions and cheese, if desired.

Calories: 495 · Protein: 32 g
Fat: 22 g/ 40% Calories from Fat · Carbohydrate: 43 g
Cholesterol: 103 mg · Sodium: 480 mg

Salisbury Steaks with Savory Sauce

Serves 4

1	POUND LEAN GROUND BEEF
4	OUNCES MUSHROOMS, COARSELY CHOPPED
2	RIBS CELERY, COARSELY CHOPPED
1	MEDIUM ONION, COARSELY CHOPPED
2	CLOVES GARLIC, MINCED
⅔	CUP FINE UNSEASONED BREADCRUMBS
½	TEASPOON SALT
¼	TEASPOON PEPPER
2	TABLESPOONS BUTTER OR MARGARINE
1	CUP BEEF BROTH, FAT REMOVED
2	TABLESPOONS TOMATO PASTE
4	TABLESPOONS CHOPPED CHIVES FOR GARNISH

1 Preheat broiler. Line broiler pan with foil.

2 In medium bowl, combine ground beef, ½ each mushrooms, celery, onion and garlic, ⅓ cup breadcrumbs, salt and pepper. Divide mixture into 4 equal portions; flatten each into a ½-inch-thick patty.

3 Place on broiler pan. Broil 4 inches from heat source for 5 minutes. Turn; broil until browned, about 7 minutes.

4 Meanwhile, in medium skillet, heat butter over medium-high heat until melted. Add remaining mushrooms, celery, onion and garlic; cook until onion is slightly softened, about 2 minutes.

5 Stir in beef broth, tomato paste and remaining ⅓ cup breadcrumbs. Bring to a boil. Reduce heat to medium-low; cover and simmer 5 minutes. Serve patties topped with vegetable sauce and chopped chives, if desired.

Calories: 380 · Protein: 25 g
Fat: 23 g/ 54% Calories from Fat · Carbohydrate: 18 g
Cholesterol: 90 mg · Sodium: 811 mg

Angel Hair Pasta with Veal, Mushrooms and Peas

Pasta isn't always topped with a tomato sauce. Here a sauce of light veal, mushrooms and peas in slightly thickened pan juices tops angel hair pasta.

Serves 4

3	TABLESPOONS ALL-PURPOSE FLOUR
1	TEASPOON DRIED OREGANO
¼	TEASPOON SALT
¼	TEASPOON PEPPER
¾	POUND VEAL CUTLETS, CUT ACROSS GRAIN INTO THIN STRIPS
2	TABLESPOONS BUTTER OR MARGARINE
2	TABLESPOONS VEGETABLE OIL
1	MEDIUM ONION, COARSELY CHOPPED
2	CLOVES GARLIC, MINCED
8	OUNCES SMALL MUSHROOMS, HALVED
1	CUP CHICKEN BROTH, FAT REMOVED
1	CUP FROZEN PEAS
8	OUNCES ANGEL HAIR OR OTHER THIN PASTA, COOKED
¼	CUP GRATED PARMESAN CHEESE (OPTIONAL)

1 In plastic or paper bag, combine flour, ½ teaspoon oregano, salt and pepper until well combined. Add veal; toss to lightly coat. Remove veal and reserve excess seasoned flour.

2 In large skillet, heat 1 tablespoon each butter and oil over medium-high heat until hot. Add veal; cook, stirring, until meat is evenly browned, about 5 minutes. Remove veal and keep warm.

3 Add remaining 1 tablespoon each butter and oil; heat until hot. Add onion and garlic; cook, stirring, until onion begins to brown, about 5 minutes.

4 Add mushrooms; cook, stirring, 1 minute. Add 1 tablespoon reserved seasoned flour; stir until well combined.

5 Add remaining ½ teaspoon oregano, broth and peas. Return veal to skillet; cook, stirring, 1 minute. Serve veal-mushroom sauce over pasta and sprinkle with cheese, if desired.

PREPARATION TIP
If desired, any long thin pasta can be used in place of angel hair pasta. Fresh angel hair pasta cooks in only 2 to 3 minutes.

Calories: 493 · Protein: 30 g
Fat: 16 g/ 29% Calories from Fat · Carbohydrate: 57 g
Cholesterol: 82 mg · Sodium: 542 mg

London Broil with Caramelized Onions

Serves 6

2 TABLESPOONS BUTTER OR MARGARINE
1 TABLESPOON OLIVE OR OTHER VEGETABLE OIL
4 MEDIUM ONIONS, SLICED
3 CLOVES GARLIC, MINCED
2 TEASPOONS SUGAR
1½ POUNDS BONELESS BEEF (LONDON BROIL)
¼ CUP BEEF BROTH
2 TABLESPOONS SHERRY OR CHICKEN BROTH
¼ TEASPOON SALT
¼ TEASPOON PEPPER

1 Preheat broiler. Line broiler pan with foil.

2 In medium skillet, heat butter and oil over medium-high heat until butter is melted.

3 Add onions and garlic; cook, stirring, until onions begin to brown, about 5 minutes. Add sugar; cook 5 minutes.

4 Meanwhile, place steak on broiler pan; broil 4 inches from heat source 8 minutes.

5 Turn; broil 7 minutes for rare, 10 minutes for medium-rare, 11 to 12 minutes for medium. Let stand 5 minutes.

6 To same skillet add beef broth and sherry. Bring to a boil.

7 Reduce heat to low; cook, stirring occasionally, until golden brown, about 15 minutes. Add salt and pepper.

8 Cut the steak into thin slices across the grain and on the diagonal. Serve steak with onions.

Calories: 271 · Protein: 23 g
Fat: 17 g/ 56% Calories from Fat · Carbohydrate: 6 g
Cholesterol: 67 mg · Sodium: 233 mg

Stovetop Barbecued Burgers

Serves 4

1 POUND LEAN GROUND BEEF
2 TEASPOONS OLIVE OR OTHER VEGETABLE OIL
2 CLOVES GARLIC, MINCED
1 MEDIUM ONION, COARSELY CHOPPED
1 CUP CRUSHED TOMATOES
¼ CUP KETCHUP
2 TABLESPOONS FROZEN ORANGE JUICE CONCENTRATE, THAWED
1 TABLESPOON CHILI POWDER
¼ TEASPOON PEPPER

1 Divide beef into 4 equal portions; flatten each into a ¾-inch-thick patty.

2 In large skillet, heat oil over medium-high heat until hot. Add patties; cook 5 minutes. Turn; cook until browned, about 4 to 6 minutes. Remove and keep warm.

3 Reduce heat to medium. To same skillet add garlic and onion; cook until onion begins to brown, about 5 minutes. Add tomatoes, ketchup, orange juice concentrate, chili powder and pepper. Increase heat to medium-high. Bring to a boil; cook 1 minute.

4 Return patties to skillet; baste with sauce. Cook until burgers are heated through, about 1 to 2 minutes.

PREPARATION TIP
If cutting down on beef is a goal, this recipe will work great with ground chicken or turkey. Be sure to use a nonstick skillet and/or spray skillet with nonstick vegetable coating.

Calories: 341 · Protein: 23 g
Fat: 22 g/ 58% Calories from Fat · Carbohydrate: 12 g
Cholesterol: 78 mg · Sodium: 278 mg

Kielbasa with Apples, Cabbage and Celery

Serves 4

1 POUND KIELBASA OR OTHER GARLIC SAUSAGE, CUT DIAGONALLY INTO ½-INCH SLICES
1 TABLESPOON PLUS 1 TEASPOON OLIVE OR OTHER VEGETABLE OIL
1 MEDIUM ONION, COARSELY CHOPPED
3 CLOVES GARLIC, MINCED
4 OUNCES CABBAGE, SHREDDED (ABOUT 3 CUPS)
2 MEDIUM GRANNY SMITH APPLES, UNPEELED, CORED, SLICED INTO ¼-INCH THICK BITE-SIZE PIECES
2 RIBS CELERY, COARSELY CHOPPED
⅓ CUP APPLE JUICE
⅓ CUP CHICKEN BROTH, FAT REMOVED
1 TABLESPOON CORNSTARCH
½ TEASPOON CRUMBLED SAGE
½ TEASPOON CELERY SEED
¼ TEASPOON PEPPER

1 In large saucepan or Dutch oven, combine kielbasa and enough water to cover over medium-high heat. Bring to a boil. Cook 3 minutes. Drain and set aside.

2 In large skillet, heat 1 tablespoon oil over medium-high heat until hot. Add onion and garlic; cook, stirring, until onion begins to brown, about 5 minutes. Add cabbage, apples and celery. Cook, stirring, until vegetables have softened, about 3 minutes. Transfer to serving platter and keep warm.

3 To same skillet add remaining 1 teaspoon oil. Add kielbasa; cook until it begins to brown, about 3 to 4 minutes.

4 Meanwhile, in small bowl, combine apple juice, broth, cornstarch, sage, celery seed and pepper. Add apple juice mixture to skillet. Bring to a boil; cook, stirring, until sauce has thickened slightly, about 2 to 3 minutes.

5 Serve kielbasa with sauce and the reserved vegetables.

Calories: 474 · Protein: 16 g
Fat: 36 g/ 68% Calories from Fat · Carbohydrate: 22 g
Cholesterol: 76 mg · Sodium: 1,327 mg

Pork Chops Diablo

Serves 4

⅓ CUP ALL-PURPOSE FLOUR
2 TABLESPOONS CHILI POWDER
¼ TEASPOON PEPPER
    PINCH CAYENNE PEPPER
4 SMALL ¼-INCH-THICK CENTER-CUT PORK CHOPS (ABOUT ¾ POUND)
2 TEASPOONS VEGETABLE OIL
1 TABLESPOON BUTTER OR MARGARINE
1 LARGE ONION, CUT INTO THIN WEDGES
1 CAN (8 OUNCES) TOMATO SAUCE
⅓ CUP BEEF BROTH
2 TEASPOONS WORCESTERSHIRE SAUCE
4 TO 5 DROPS HOT PEPPER SAUCE
1 TEASPOON DRY MUSTARD

1 In plastic or paper bag, combine flour, chili powder, pepper and cayenne until well mixed. Add pork chops; toss to evenly coat. Remove chops and reserve 1 tablespoon seasoned flour.

2 In large skillet, heat oil over medium-high heat until hot. Add pork chops; cook, turning once, until browned, about 6 to 8 minutes. Remove and keep warm.

3 To same skillet add butter and onion; cook until onion begins to brown, about 3 minutes.

4 Stir in the reserved 1 tablespoon seasoned flour; cook until well incorporated, about 30 seconds. Add tomato sauce, broth, Worcestershire sauce, hot pepper sauce and mustard.

5 Add any juices from pork chops into onion-tomato sauce; bring to a boil, stirring constantly. Add pork chops. Reduce heat to low; cover and simmer, turning once, until chops are cooked through, about 12 minutes.

Calories: 253 · Protein: 22 g
Fat: 12 g/ 42% Calories from Fat · Carbohydrate: 15 g
Cholesterol: 61 mg · Sodium: 549 mg

Spicy Lamb Sauté

Serves 4

1 POUND BONELESS LAMB (LEG OR LOIN), CUT INTO 2-INCH BY ¼-INCH SLICES
¼ CUP PLUS 2 TABLESPOONS CORNSTARCH
2 TABLESPOONS OLIVE OR OTHER VEGETABLE OIL
3 SLICES ¼-INCH-THICK FRESH GINGER, MINCED
3 CLOVES GARLIC, MINCED
1 LARGE RED PEPPER, CUT INTO ¾-INCH PIECES
1 PACKAGE (10 OUNCES) FROZEN GREEN BEANS
⅔ CUP BEEF BROTH, FAT REMOVED
2 TABLESPOONS REDUCED-SODIUM SOY SAUCE
1 TABLESPOON RED WINE OR CIDER VINEGAR
½ TEASPOON SUGAR
¼ TEASPOON RED PEPPER FLAKES
8 OUNCES BOW TIE PASTA, COOKED, HOT

1 In plastic or paper bag, combine lamb and the ¼ cup cornstarch; toss to evenly coat. In large skillet, heat 1 tablespoon oil over medium-high heat until hot. Add lamb; cook, stirring, until lamb begins to brown, about 4 minutes. Remove lamb and keep warm.

2 To same skillet add remaining 1 tablespoon oil. Add ginger and garlic; cook, stirring constantly, until garlic starts to brown, about 1 to 2 minutes.

3 Add red pepper, green beans, ⅓ cup broth, soy sauce, vinegar, sugar and red pepper flakes. Bring to a boil. Add lamb.

4 In small bowl, combine remaining ⅓ cup broth and remaining 2 tablespoons cornstarch. Add to skillet with lamb-vegetable mixture. Return mixture to a boil, stirring constantly until thickened, about 2 to 3 minutes. Serve over cooked pasta.

Calories: 488 · Protein: 33 g
Fat: 13 g/ 23% Calories from Fat · Carbohydrate: 58 g
Cholesterol: 73 mg · Sodium: 516 mg

Cheese-Filled Pepper Burger

Serves 4

1 POUND GROUND BEEF ROUND
1 MEDIUM ONION, FINELY CHOPPED
2 TABLESPOONS WORCESTERSHIRE OR STEAK SAUCE
1 TEASPOON COARSELY CRACKED PEPPER
½ TEASPOON SALT
4 OUNCES MONTEREY JACK OR PEPPER JACK CHEESE, SHREDDED

1 In medium bowl, combine beef, onion, Worcestershire sauce, ¼ teaspoon pepper and salt; toss to evenly combine. Divide mixture into 4 equal portions; flatten each into a patty.

2 Press ¼ cheese into center of each patty, working meat to totally enclose cheese. Sprinkle patties with remaining pepper, pressing it gently into meat.

3 In large nonstick or cast-iron skillet, over medium-high heat, cook patties, turning once, until of desired doneness, 6 minutes for medium-rare, 4 minutes for medium and 10 minutes for well done.

PREPARATION TIP
If desired, the coated, stuffed burgers can be broiled or grilled instead of pan-fried.

Calories: 338 · Protein: 29 g
Fat: 23 g/ 61% Calories from Fat · Carbohydrate: 3 g
Cholesterol: 94 mg · Sodium: 568 mg

Sweet-and-Sour Mustard Scallopini

Serves 4

⅓ CUP ALL-PURPOSE FLOUR
½ TEASPOON SALT
¼ TEASPOON PEPPER
8 VEAL SCALLOPINI (ABOUT 1 POUND)
2 TABLESPOONS BUTTER OR MARGARINE
2 TABLESPOONS OLIVE OR OTHER VEGETABLE OIL
½ CUP BEER
½ CUP CHICKEN BROTH, FAT REMOVED
2 TABLESPOONS SPICY BROWN MUSTARD
2 TABLESPOONS BROWN SUGAR
1 TEASPOON DRY MUSTARD
1 TEASPOON DRIED THYME
3 TABLESPOONS LEMON JUICE
1½ TEASPOONS GRATED LEMON PEEL

1 In plastic or paper bag, combine flour, salt and pepper. Add veal; toss to lightly coat. Remove veal; reserve seasoned flour.

2 In large skillet, heat 1 tablespoon each butter and oil over medium-high heat until butter is melted. Add veal; cook, turning once, until brown, about 4 minutes; add 1 tablespoon oil to prevent sticking. Remove veal and keep warm.

3 To same skillet add remaining 1 tablespoon butter. Stir in reserved seasoned flour; cook until well incorporated, about 30 seconds.

4 Stir in beer, broth, brown mustard, sugar, dry mustard and thyme. Bring to a boil, stirring constantly. Cook until slightly thickened, about 1 to 2 minutes.

5 Stir in lemon juice and peel. Return reserved veal to skillet. Bring to a boil. Reduce heat to low; cover and simmer until veal is cooked through, about 1 to 2 minutes.

Pork Satay with Dipping Sauce

Serves 4

1 POUND BONELESS PORK LOIN, HALVED LENGTHWISE, CUT INTO THIN STRIPS
3 TABLESPOONS REDUCED-SODIUM SOY SAUCE
1 TABLESPOON ORIENTAL SESAME OIL
2 TEASPOONS HONEY
3 CLOVES GARLIC, MINCED
6 SLICES ¼-INCH-THICK FRESH GINGER, MINCED
1 TEASPOON GROUND CORIANDER
¼ CUP CREAMY PEANUT BUTTER
3 TABLESPOONS CHICKEN BROTH, FAT REMOVED
1 TABLESPOON RICE WINE OR WHITE VINEGAR

1 Preheat broiler. Line broiler pan with foil. On skewers, thread pork strips; place on broiler pan.

2 In small bowl or container, combine soy sauce, 2 teaspoons sesame oil, honey, garlic, ½ ginger and coriander. Brush generously on pork.

3 Broil 4 inches from heat source, turning once, until pork is cooked through, about 8 to 12 minutes.

4 Meanwhile, in small bowl, combine peanut butter, broth, vinegar, remaining 1 teaspoon sesame oil and remaining ginger until well mixed. Pour in 3 tablespoons cooked pork pan juices, additional broth or water until of desired consistency.

5 Serve skewered pork with peanut sauce.

Calories: 324 · Protein: 26 g
Fat: 15 g/ 41% Calories from Fat · Carbohydrate: 17 g
Cholesterol: 104 mg · Sodium: 609 mg

Calories: 402 · Protein: 27 g
Fat: 29 g/ 64% Calories from Fat · Carbohydrate: 8 g
Cholesterol: 77 mg · Sodium: 629 mg

Spaghetti and Little Meatballs

Serves 4

1	TABLESPOON OLIVE OR OTHER VEGETABLE OIL
1	MEDIUM ONION, MINCED
2	CLOVES GARLIC, MINCED
¼	POUND LEAN GROUND BEEF ROUND
¼	POUND LEAN GROUND PORK
3	TABLESPOONS CHOPPED FRESH PARSLEY
½	TEASPOON DRIED OREGANO
½	TEASPOON SALT
¼	TEASPOON DRIED SAGE
¼	TEASPOON PEPPER
2	SLICES WHITE BREAD, CRUMBLED
3	TABLESPOONS LOW-FAT (1%) MILK
⅓	CUP GRATED PARMESAN CHEESE
1	EGG WHITE
1	CAN (14½ OUNCES) NO-SALT-ADDED STEWED TOMATOES, BROKEN UP
1	CAN (8 OUNCES) NO-SALT-ADDED TOMATO SAUCE
10	OUNCES SPAGHETTI

1 In large pot, bring to a boil enough water to cook pasta over medium-high heat.

2 In large nonstick skillet, heat oil over medium heat until hot. Add onion and garlic; cook, stirring frequently, until onion begins to soften, about 5 minutes. Transfer to large bowl.

3 To onion add ground beef and pork, parsley, oregano, salt, sage and pepper; mix well. Add bread, milk, 3 tablespoons Parmesan cheese and egg white; mix until well combined. Shape into 32 small (walnut size) meatballs.

4 In same skillet, combine tomatoes and tomato sauce over medium heat. Bring to a boil. Reduce heat to low; add meatballs. Cover and simmer until meatballs are cooked through, about 7 minutes.

5 Meanwhile, add spaghetti to boiling water; cook until al dente, about 8 to 12 minutes. Drain. Serve spaghetti topped with meatballs and sauce sprinkled with remaining Parmesan cheese.

Calories: 547 · Protein: 27 g
Fat: 15 g/ 24% Calories from Fat · Carbohydrate: 76 g
Cholesterol: 44 mg · Sodium: 570 mg

Pork with Apple-Caraway Cream

Serves 4

4	BONELESS PORK CHOPS (ABOUT ¾ POUND)
2	TABLESPOONS ALL-PURPOSE FLOUR
1	TABLESPOON VEGETABLE OIL
2	MEDIUM ONIONS, CUT INTO THIN WEDGES
3	CLOVES GARLIC, MINCED
1	TABLESPOON BUTTER OR MARGARINE
¼	CUP DRY WHITE WINE
¼	CUP BEEF BROTH
1	TABLESPOON DIJON MUSTARD
1	TEASPOON CARAWAY SEEDS
¼	TEASPOON DRY MUSTARD
½	TEASPOON SALT
¼	TEASPOON PEPPER
1	RED APPLE, CUT INTO THIN WEDGES
¼	CUP SOUR CREAM

1 In shallow dish, coat pork with flour; remove pork and reserve excess flour.

2 In large nonstick skillet, heat 2 teaspoons oil over medium-high heat until hot. Add onions and garlic; cook, stirring constantly, until onions begin to brown, about 3 to 5 minutes. Remove onions.

3 To same skillet add remaining 1 teaspoon oil. Add pork; cook, turning once, until browned, 6 to 8 minutes. Remove pork and keep warm.

4 To same skillet add butter; cook until melted. Add reserved flour; cook, stirring, until well incorporated, about 30 seconds. Stir in wine, broth, Dijon mustard, caraway seeds, dry mustard, salt and pepper. Bring to a boil.

5 Add reserved onions, reserved pork and apple. Reduce heat to low; cover and simmer, turning once, until pork is cooked through, about 7 minutes.

6 Transfer pork to serving platter. Stir sour cream into sauce and serve.

Calories: 390 · Protein: 17 g
Fat: 28 g/ 64% Calories from Fat · Carbohydrate: 14 g
Cholesterol: 74 mg · Sodium: 524 mg

Chinese Hot Pot

Serves 4

2	TEASPOONS ORIENTAL SESAME OIL
5	SLICES ¼-INCH-THICK FRESH GINGER, FINELY CHOPPED
3	CLOVES GARLIC, MINCED
4	OUNCES LEAN GROUND PORK, CRUMBLED
1	CAN (19 OUNCES) CHICKPEAS, RINSED, DRAINED
2½	CUPS CHICKEN BROTH, FAT REMOVED
1	CAN (8 OUNCES) SLICED BAMBOO SHOOTS, DRAINED
1	CAN (8 OUNCES) SLICED WATER CHESTNUTS, DRAINED
1	TABLESPOON REDUCED-SODIUM SOY SAUCE
2	DROPS HOT PEPPER SAUCE
½	TEASPOON RED PEPPER FLAKES
2	TABLESPOONS CORNSTARCH
4	OUNCES FIRM TOFU, CUT INTO ½-INCH CUBES
4	OUNCES FRESH OR FROZEN SNOW PEAS, TRIMMED
¼	CUP PACKED CILANTRO SPRIGS, FINELY CHOPPED (OPTIONAL)

1 In large saucepan or Dutch oven, heat sesame oil over medium-high heat until hot. Add ginger and garlic; cook, stirring constantly, 1 minute.

2 Add crumbled pork; cook, stirring constantly, until meat begins to brown, about 3 minutes.

3 Add chickpeas, 2 cups broth, bamboo shoots, water chestnuts, soy sauce, hot pepper sauce and red pepper flakes. Reduce heat to medium; bring to a boil.

4 In small bowl, combine remaining ½ cup broth and cornstarch until well mixed. Add broth mixture, tofu and snow peas. Cook until slightly thickened and snow peas are cooked through, about 4 minutes. Stir in cilantro, if desired.

Calories: 278 · Protein: 13 g
Fat: 12 g/ 38% Calories from Fat · Carbohydrate: 30 g
Cholesterol: 21 mg · Sodium: 942 mg

Pork and Linguine Stir-Fry

*This colorful, flavorful, takeoff on the Chinese lo mein noodle dish
makes a great complete meal eaten hot, or at room temperature for picnic fare.*

Serves 4

1 CUP REDUCED-SODIUM CHICKEN BROTH,
FAT REMOVED

2½ TABLESPOONS REDUCED-SODIUM SOY SAUCE

2 TABLESPOONS RICE WINE OR CIDER VINEGAR

4 TEASPOONS CORNSTARCH

6 OUNCES BONELESS PORK LOIN,
CUT INTO 2-INCH BY ¼-INCH STRIPS

1 TABLESPOON PLUS 2 TEASPOONS PEANUT OIL

1 RED PEPPER, CUT INTO THIN STRIPS

2 CUPS ¼-INCH-THICK
SHREDDED NAPA CABBAGE

4 CLOVES GARLIC, MINCED

⅓ CUP CHOPPED GREEN ONIONS

2 TABLESPOONS MINCED FRESH GINGER

8 OUNCES SNOW PEAS, TRIMMED,
CUT IN HALF LENGTHWISE

½ CUP SLICED WATER CHESTNUTS

3 TABLESPOONS CHOPPED FRESH CILANTRO
OR PARSLEY

10 OUNCES WHOLE-WHEAT LINGUINE,
COOKED, HOT

1 In small bowl or container, combine broth, soy sauce and vinegar until well mixed; set aside. In plastic or paper bag, place 2 teaspoons cornstarch. Add pork; toss to evenly coat.

2 In large nonstick skillet, heat 1 tablespoon oil over medium heat until hot. Add pork; cook, stirring frequently, until golden brown, about 3 minutes. Remove and keep warm.

3 To same skillet add red pepper; cook 1 minute. Add cabbage; cook, stirring frequently, until crisp-tender, about 3 minutes.

4 Add garlic, green onions and ginger; cook until fragrant, about 1 minute. Add snow peas and water chestnuts; cook until snow peas are crisp-tender, about 2 minutes.

5 Increase heat to medium-high. Add reserved broth mixture. Bring to a boil. In cup, combine remaining 2 teaspoons cornstarch and 1 tablespoon water until well mixed; stir into vegetable mixture. Cook, stirring constantly until slightly thickened, about 1 minute.

6 Reduce heat to medium-low. Add pork, cook until cooked through, about 1 minute. Stir in cilantro.

7 In large serving bowl, combine the pork-vegetable sauce and linguine; toss gently to evenly coat.

PREPARATION TIP
For an easy way to shred napa cabbage, remove individual leaves, stack in piles of four or five leaves and thinly slice ¼ inch thick with a large chef's knife.

Calories: 437 · Protein: 24 g
Fat: 9 g/ 18% Calories from Fat · Carbohydrate: 69 g
Cholesterol: 27 mg · Sodium: 578 mg

Spicy Fajita Roll-Ups

Serves 4

- **3** TABLESPOONS CIDER VINEGAR
- **1** TEASPOON HONEY
- **1** TABLESPOON VEGETABLE OIL
- **3** CLOVES GARLIC, MINCED
- **2** TABLESPOONS CHILI POWDER
- **1** TABLESPOON CUMIN
- **¼** TEASPOON RED PEPPER FLAKES
- **1** POUND BEEF FLANK STEAK
- **1** LARGE ONION, HALVED LENGTHWISE, CUT CROSSWISE INTO THIN SLICES
- **1** LARGE RED PEPPER, CUT INTO THIN STRIPS
- **8** LARGE BOSTON OR BIBB LETTUCE LEAVES
- **¾** CUP PLAIN YOGURT

1 Preheat broiler. Line broiler pan with foil. In shallow container or baking dish large enough to hold steak, combine vinegar and honey until well mixed. Add oil, garlic, chili powder, cumin and red pepper flakes. Add flank steak; turn to coat and set aside.

2 Place steak on broiler pan, reserving remaining marinade. Broil 4 inches from heat source 7 minutes. Turn; broil until medium-rare, about 6 to 8 minutes. Let stand 5 minutes. Thinly slice across the grain; reserve pan juices.

3 In medium skillet, place reserved marinade over medium heat; cook until bubbly. Add onion and pepper; cook, stirring constantly, 1 minute. Reduce heat to low; cover and simmer until vegetables are crisp-tender, about 6 minutes. Add reserved pan juices.

4 To serve, place 2 lettuce leaves on each of our plates. Divide steak and onion-pepper mixture among plates; top with a dollop of yogurt.

Orange Pork Stir-Fry

Serves 4

- **1** POUND BONELESS PORK LOIN, HALVED LENGTHWISE, CUT INTO THIN STRIPS
- **3** TABLESPOONS PEANUT OR OTHER VEGETABLE OIL
- **2** TABLESPOONS REDUCED-SODIUM SOY SAUCE
- **1** TABLESPOON PLUS 2 TEASPOONS CORNSTARCH
- **¾** CUP BEEF BROTH, FAT REMOVED
- **2** TABLESPOONS KETCHUP
- **1** TEASPOON GRATED ORANGE PEEL (OPTIONAL)
- **3** SLICES ¼-INCH-THICK FRESH GINGER (OPTIONAL)
- **1** LARGE GREEN PEPPER, CUT INTO 1-INCH PIECES
- **6** TO 8 GREEN ONIONS, CUT INTO 2-INCH PIECES
- **1** CAN (11 OUNCES) MANDARIN ORANGES, DRAINED

1 In medium bowl, combine pork strips, 1 tablespoon each oil, soy sauce and cornstarch until well mixed. Set aside.

2 In small bowl, combine remaining 1 tablespoon soy sauce, remaining 2 teaspoons cornstarch, broth, ketchup and orange peel, if desired, until well mixed.

3 In large skillet or wok, heat 1 tablespoon oil over medium-high heat until hot. Add pork, marinade and ginger, if desired; cook, stirring constantly, until browned yet slightly pink in center, about 3 to 4 minutes. Remove and keep warm.

4 In same skillet add remaining 1 tablespoon oil; add green pepper and green onions; cook, stirring constantly, until green onions wilt, about 3 to 4 minutes. Return pork.

5 Stir reserved broth mixture; add to skillet. Bring to a boil, stirring. Add oranges; cook, stirring constantly, until pork is cooked through, about 2 to 3 minutes. Discard ginger slices, if used.

Calories: 296 · Protein: 25 g
Fat: 17 g/ 51% Calories from Fat · Carbohydrate: 12 g
Cholesterol: 60 mg · Sodium: 135 mg

Calories: 358 · Protein: 26 g
Fat: 19 g/ 47% Calories from Fat · Carbohydrate: 22 g
Cholesterol: 68 mg · Sodium: 623 mg

Oriental Noodle Soup

Serves 4

5 CUPS CHICKEN BROTH

2 CUPS WATER

4 SLICES ¼-INCH-THICK FRESH GINGER

½ TEASPOON ORIENTAL SESAME OIL

½ POUND ANGEL HAIR PASTA (CAPELLINI)

1 THICK SLICE HAM (ABOUT ¼ POUND), CUT INTO 2-INCH BY ¼-INCH STRIPS

4 LETTUCE LEAVES, SHREDDED

2 MEDIUM ZUCCHINI (ABOUT ¾ POUND), CUT INTO 2-INCH BY ¼-INCH STRIPS

4 MEDIUM CARROTS, CUT INTO 2-INCH BY ¼-INCH STRIPS

1 In large saucepan or Dutch oven, combine broth, water, ginger and sesame oil. Bring to a boil over medium-high heat.

2 Add the pasta and cook until just barely al dente, about 5 to 7 minutes.

3 Arrange the ham and vegetables on top of soup, covering one-quarter of the surface with each ingredient. Cover and cook until lettuce is wilted and ham heated through, about 2 to 3 minutes.

PREPARATION TIP
If desired, chicken, turkey or beef can be substituted for ham for variation.

Calories: 332 · Protein: 17 g
Fat: 5 g/ 13% Calories from Fat · Carbohydrate: 56 g
Cholesterol: 13 mg · Sodium: 1,690 mg

Simple Beef Burgundy

Serves 4

1 POUND BEEF FLANK STEAK, HALVED LENGTHWISE, CUT ACROSS GRAIN INTO ¼-INCH-THICK SLICES

½ CUP DRY RED WINE

4 TABLESPOONS BUTTER OR MARGARINE

2 CLOVES GARLIC, MINCED

½ POUND MUSHROOMS, CUT INTO ¼-INCH SLICES

6 TO 8 GREEN ONIONS, CUT INTO 2-INCH PIECES

2 TABLESPOONS ALL-PURPOSE FLOUR

½ TEASPOON SALT

¼ TEASPOON PEPPER

¼ CUP BEEF BROTH, FAT REMOVED

1 TEASPOON DRIED TARRAGON

¼ CUP CHOPPED PARSLEY (OPTIONAL)

1 In medium bowl, combine beef slices and wine; let stand.

2 In large skillet, heat 2 tablespoons butter over medium heat until melted. Add garlic, mushrooms and green onions; cook, stirring constantly, until mushrooms are limp, about 5 minutes. Remove with pan juices and set aside.

3 Drain beef, reserving marinade. In plastic or paper bag, combine flour, salt and pepper until well mixed. Add drained beef; toss to evenly coat.

4 In same skillet, wiped dry, heat remaining 2 tablespoons butter over medium-high heat until melted. Add beef; cook, stirring constantly, until browned, about 3 to 4 minutes.

5 Add reserved vegetables and liquid, reserved marinade, broth and tarragon. Bring to a boil; cook, stirring, until thickened, about 1 to 2 minutes. Sprinkle with parsley, if desired.

Calories: 324 · Protein: 26 g
Fat: 21 g/ 58% Calories from Fat · Carbohydrate: 8 g
Cholesterol: 99 mg · Sodium: 510 mg

SEAFOOD AND FISH

Grilled Salmon with Green Sauce

This delicious mustard-lemon basted salmon is equally good when broiled indoors or pan-fried in a hot skillet.

Serves 4

- **4** SALMON STEAKS ABOUT 1 INCH THICK (ABOUT 8 OUNCES EACH)
- **3** TABLESPOONS OLIVE OR OTHER VEGETABLE OIL
- **2** TABLESPOONS DIJON MUSTARD
- **2** TABLESPOONS LEMON JUICE
- **2** TEASPOONS GRATED LEMON PEEL (OPTIONAL)
- **3** CLOVES GARLIC, MINCED
- **½** TEASPOON SALT
- **¼** TEASPOON PEPPER
- **¼** CUP PACKED FRESH BASIL LEAVES
- **¼** CUP PACKED DILL SPRIGS
- **¼** CUP PACKED PARSLEY SPRIGS
- **4** OUNCES SPINACH, TRIMMED
- **¼** CUP PLAIN YOGURT

1 Preheat broiler or grill according to manufacturer's directions. If broiling, place salmon on broiler rack; set aside.

2 In small bowl, blend oil, mustard, lemon juice, lemon peel, if desired, garlic, salt and pepper until well mixed. Set aside 1 tablespoon for basting salmon.

3 In food processor or blender, process basil, dill and parsley until minced. Add spinach; process until puréed and smooth. Add yogurt. With machine running, gradually add oil mixture; process until thick mayonnaise consistency. Refrigerate.

4 Lightly brush salmon with half reserved oil mixture. Grill or broil 4 inches from heat source 6 minutes. Turn; brush with remaining oil mixture; grill or broil until fish flakes easily when tested with a fork, about 6 minutes.

5 Serve with green sauce.

PREPARATION TIP

"Sauce Verde," or green sauce, can be made with a variety of fresh herbs and greens—basil, dill, parsley, cilantro, chives, watercress, spinach, arugula, etc.

Calories: 411 · Protein: 42 g
Fat: 24 g/ 52% Calories from Fat · Carbohydrate: 6 g
Cholesterol: 111 mg · Sodium: 625 mg

All-American Shrimp Salad

Serves 4

1¼	POUNDS ALL-PURPOSE POTATOES, PEELED, CUT INTO ½-INCH CUBES
1	CUP REDUCED-SODIUM CHICKEN BROTH, FAT REMOVED
2	CLOVES GARLIC, MINCED
1	POUND MEDIUM SHRIMP, SHELLED AND DEVEINED
¾	CUP PLAIN NONFAT YOGURT
3	TABLESPOONS REDUCED-FAT MAYONNAISE
2	TABLESPOONS LEMON JUICE
½	TEASPOON DRIED TARRAGON
½	TEASPOON SALT
¼	TEASPOON PEPPER
3	GREEN ONIONS, THINLY SLICED
1	RED PEPPER, CUT INTO ½-INCH PIECES
	LETTUCE LEAVES FOR GARNISH

1 In large pot, combine potatoes and enough water to cover over medium-high heat. Bring to a boil; cook until firm-tender, about 7 minutes. Drain.

2 Meanwhile, in large skillet, combine broth and garlic over medium-high heat. Bring to a boil. Reduce heat to low. Add shrimp; cook until shrimp are opaque, about 4 minutes. Drain, reserving ⅓ cup cooking liquid. When cool enough to handle, halve shrimp crosswise.

3 In large bowl, combine reserved cooking liquid, yogurt, mayonnaise, lemon juice, tarragon, salt and pepper. Add cooked potatoes, shrimp, green onions and red pepper; toss gently to evenly coat. Serve over lettuce, if desired.

Calories: 260 · Protein: 25 g
Fat: 4 g/ 13% Calories from Fat · Carbohydrate: 31 g
Cholesterol: 141 mg · Sodium: 615 mg

Foil-Baked Sole and Vegetables

Serves 4

4	BONELESS FILLETS OF SOLE (ABOUT 1½ POUNDS)
4	GREEN ONIONS, COARSELY CHOPPED
1	LARGE CARROT, THINLY SLICED
1	RIB CELERY, THINLY SLICED
⅓	CUP BUTTER OR MARGARINE, AT ROOM TEMPERATURE
3	TABLESPOONS CHOPPED PARSLEY (OPTIONAL)
1	CLOVE GARLIC, MINCED
½	TEASPOON TARRAGON
¼	TEASPOON SALT
¼	TEASPOON PEPPER

1 Preheat oven to 425°. Cut four 12-inch squares heavy-duty foil; set aside. Place one fish fillet in center of each. Top each with equal amounts green onions, carrot and celery.

2 In small bowl, combine butter, parsley, if desired, garlic, tarragon, salt and pepper until well mixed. Place ¼ butter mixture in each packet.

3 Tightly seal. Place packets on baking sheet. Bake until fish flakes easily when tested with fork, about 12 minutes.

PREPARATION TIP
To cook in the microwave, place the fish in a single layer in microwave-safe baking dish; top with vegetables and seasoned butter as above. Cover with plastic wrap, vented at corner. Cook on High (100% power), rotating dish once, 7 minutes. Let stand, covered, 3 minutes.

Calories: 307 · Protein: 33 g
Fat: 17 g/ 49% Calories from Fat · Carbohydrate: 4 g
Cholesterol: 123 mg · Sodium: 446 mg

Swordfish Skewers with Garlic-Lime Marinade

Serves 4

1 LARGE OR 2 SMALL LIMES
4 TABLESPOONS OLIVE OR OTHER VEGETABLE OIL
2 TABLESPOONS TOMATO PASTE
2 TEASPOONS DRY MUSTARD
4 CLOVES GARLIC, MINCED
1 TEASPOON SALT
½ TEASPOON SUGAR
½ TEASPOON PEPPER
1 POUND BONELESS SWORDFISH, CUT INTO 24 EQUAL PIECES
1 LARGE RED ONION, HALVED, CUT INTO QUARTERS
1 LARGE YELLOW OR GREEN PEPPER, CUT INTO 16 SQUARES, (1 INCH)
12 CHERRY TOMATOES

1 Preheat broiler or grill according to manufacturer's directions. Grate lime peel to measure 2 teaspoons. Juice limes to measure 3 tablespoons. Set aside.

2 In small bowl, combine lime peel, lime juice, oil, tomato paste, dry mustard, garlic, salt, sugar and pepper.

3 On 8 skewers, thread swordfish, onions, yellow pepper and tomatoes.

4 Brush with lime-oil mixture. Place on grill or broiler pan.

5 Grill or broil 4 inches from heat source 5 minutes.

6 Turn; brush with remaining lime-oil mixture; grill or broil until fish is cooked through, about 5 minutes.

Pecan-Crusted Snapper

Serves 4

1 GREEN ONION, MINCED
½ CUP CHOPPED PECANS (ABOUT 2 OUNCES)
2 TABLESPOONS FINE UNSEASONED BREADCRUMBS
¼ CUP ALL-PURPOSE FLOUR
1 TEASPOON SALT
½ TEASPOON PEPPER
1 EGG
1 TABLESPOON MILK
4 RED SNAPPER FILLETS OR OTHER FIRM-FLESHED WHITE FISH (ABOUT 1 POUND)
1 TABLESPOON BUTTER OR MARGARINE
1 TABLESPOON VEGETABLE OIL

1 In shallow bowl or deep plate, combine green onions, pecans and breadcrumbs until well mixed. In another shallow bowl or deep plate, combine flour, salt and pepper until well mixed. In third shallow bowl or deep plate, combine egg and milk until well mixed.

2 Place fish in flour mixture, then egg mixture and finally in pecan mixture to coat well.

3 In large nonstick skillet, heat butter and oil over medium-high heat until butter is melted. Add coated fish; cook, turning once, until golden and fish flakes easily when tested with fork, about 6 minutes.

PREPARATION TIP
Be sure each coating completely covers the fish to lock in the fish juices for extra moistness.

Calories: 304 · Protein: 24 g
Fat: 19 g/ 56% Calories from Fat · Carbohydrate: 10 g
Cholesterol: 44 mg · Sodium: 722 mg

Calories: 327 · Protein: 27 g
Fat: 19 g/ 52% Calories from Fat · Carbohydrate: 12 g
Cholesterol: 104 mg · Sodium: 693 mg

Sole with Cucumber-Dill Sauce

The sauce is given a tangy twist by using yogurt in the place of mayonnaise.
Use low- or non-fat yogurt to save calories.

Serves 4

4 SMALL FILLETS OF SOLE OR OTHER FIRM-
FLESHED WHITE FISH (ABOUT 1½ POUNDS)

¼ CUP PACKED FRESH OR
1½ TEASPOONS DRIED DILL

1 TABLESPOON BUTTER OR MARGARINE, MELTED

½ TEASPOON SALT

½ TEASPOON PEPPER

1 CUP PLAIN YOGURT

3 TABLESPOONS LEMON JUICE

2 TEASPOONS GRATED LEMON PEEL
(OPTIONAL)

½ TEASPOON DRY MUSTARD

1 CHUNK CUCUMBER, 2 INCHES LONG, PEELED,
FINELY CHOPPED

¼ CUP MINCED RED PEPPER (SMALL)

1 Preheat broiler. Line broiler pan with foil; lightly grease. Place fish on broiler pan; set aside.

2 In small bowl, combine 1 tablespoon fresh dill, butter, ¼ teaspoon salt and ¼ teaspoon pepper. Brush over fish. Broil 4 inches from heat source 3 minutes. Turn; brush with additional dill-butter. Broil until fish flakes easily when tested with fork, about 4 to 6 minutes.

3 In medium bowl, combine remaining 3 tablespoons fresh dill, ¼ teaspoon salt, ¼ teaspoon pepper, yogurt, lemon juice, lemon peel, if desired, and mustard. Stir in cucumber and red pepper.

4 Serve fish topped with cucumber sauce.

Calories: 226 · Protein: 35 g
Fat: 6 g/ 23% Calories from Fat · Carbohydrate: 6 g
Cholesterol: 93 mg · Sodium: 488 mg

Shrimp Lo Mein

Serves 4

2 TABLESPOONS REDUCED-SODIUM SOY SAUCE
2 TABLESPOONS DRY SHERRY
2 TEASPOONS ORIENTAL SESAME OIL
1 TEASPOON CORNSTARCH
¾ POUND MEDIUM SHRIMP, SHELLED AND DEVEINED
1 TABLESPOON VEGETABLE OIL
3 SLICES ¼-INCH-THICK FRESH GINGER, MINCED
3 GREEN ONIONS, MINCED
2 CARROTS, DICED
1 LARGE LEEK, HALVED LENGTHWISE, CUT INTO 2-INCH STRIPS
½ CUP SLICED WATER CHESTNUTS
½ CUP BABY CORN
½ CUP FROZEN GREEN PEAS
¼ CUP CHILI SAUCE
⅔ CUP REDUCED-SODIUM CHICKEN BROTH, FAT REMOVED
8 OUNCES FETTUCCINE, COOKED

1 In medium bowl, combine soy sauce, sherry, sesame oil and cornstarch. Add shrimp; toss to evenly coat and set aside.

2 In large nonstick skillet, heat oil until hot over medium heat. Add ginger and green onions; cook, stirring frequently, until fragrant, about 1 minute. Stir in carrots and leeks; cook, stirring frequently, until vegetables are almost tender, about 3 minutes.

3 To vegetable mixture in same skillet, add shrimp and marinade; cook, stirring constantly, until shrimp are almost opaque, about 2 minutes.

4 Stir in water chestnuts, baby corn, peas and chili sauce until well mixed. Add broth. Increase heat to high; cook, stirring constantly, until shrimp is cooked through, about 1 minute.

5 In large serving bowl, combine fettuccine and shrimp mixture; toss gently to evenly coat.

Calories: 469 · Protein: 27 g
Fat: 10 g/ 19% Calories from Fat · Carbohydrate: 67 g
Cholesterol: 159 mg · Sodium: 801 mg

Red Snapper with Orange Sauce

Serves 4

2 TABLESPOONS ALL-PURPOSE FLOUR
¾ TEASPOON SALT
⅜ TEASPOON PEPPER
2 FILLETS ¾-INCH-THICK RED SNAPPER (ABOUT 1 POUND), HALVED
1 TABLESPOON OLIVE OR OTHER VEGETABLE OIL
4 TABLESPOONS BUTTER OR MARGARINE, AT ROOM TEMPERATURE
1 TABLESPOON FROZEN ORANGE JUICE CONCENTRATE, THAWED
1 TEASPOON CHILI POWDER
2 TABLESPOONS CHOPPED PARSLEY (OPTIONAL)

1 In plastic or paper bag or shallow dish, combine flour, ½ teaspoon salt and ¼ teaspoon pepper. Add fish; toss to lightly coat.

2 In large nonstick skillet, heat oil over medium-high heat until hot. Add fish; cook, turning once, until fish flakes easily when tested with fork, about 6 to 8 minutes.

3 Meanwhile, to make orange sauce, in small bowl, combine remaining ¼ teaspoon salt, ⅛ teaspoon pepper, butter, orange juice concentrate and chili powder until well mixed.

4 Serve fish topped with orange sauce and parsley, if desired.

PREPARATION TIP
Make the spicy orange butter ahead and keep refrigerated. Or double or triple the quantities, form into a roll, tightly seal in plastic wrap and freeze. To use, slice off what's needed.

Calories: 269 · Protein: 24 g
Fat: 17 g/ 56% Calories from Fat · Carbohydrate: 5 g
Cholesterol: 73 mg · Sodium: 608 mg

Tuna-Rice Salad

The longest and most difficult part of making this light supper dish is cooking the rice!

Serves 6

1	CUP LOW-SODIUM CHICKEN BROTH
1	CUP WATER
1	CUP LONG-GRAIN RICE
2	CLOVES GARLIC, MINCED
⅓	CUP LEMON JUICE
¼	CUP OLIVE OR OTHER VEGETABLE OIL
1	TABLESPOON DIJON MUSTARD
¼	TEASPOON SALT
½	TEASPOON PEPPER
1	CAN (6½ OUNCES) WATER-PACKED TUNA, DRAINED
1	LARGE YELLOW OR GREEN PEPPER, CUT INTO BITE-SIZE PIECES
1	PINT CHERRY TOMATOES, HALVED
4	GREEN ONIONS, COARSELY CHOPPED
¼	CUP CHOPPED FRESH OR 2 TEASPOONS DRIED DILL
1	SMALL HEAD BOSTON OR ICEBERG LETTUCE, SEPARATED INTO LEAVES

1 In medium saucepan, combine broth and water over medium-high heat; bring to a boil. Add rice and garlic. Reduce heat to low; cover and simmer until rice is tender and liquid is absorbed, about 15 to 20 minutes. Turn into large serving bowl and set aside.

2 To make dressing, in small bowl, combine lemon juice, oil, mustard, salt and pepper.

3 To cooled rice add tuna, yellow pepper, tomatoes, green onions, dill and dressing; toss gently to evenly coat.

4 Serve on lettuce leaves.

PREPARATION TIP

It isn't faster, but to keep the kitchen cool in the summer, cook the rice in the microwave. In shallow 2-quart microwave-safe casserole combine broth, 1 cup hot water, rice and garlic. Cover and cook on High (100% power) 8 minutes. Cook on Medium (50% power) 12 minutes or until rice is tender.

Calories: 258 · Protein: 12 g
Fat: 10 g/ 34% Calories from Fat · Carbohydrate: 30 g
Cholesterol: 12 mg · Sodium: 282 mg

Sautéed Sesame Fish

Serves 4

¼	CUP ALL-PURPOSE FLOUR
1	TEASPOON SALT
¼	TEASPOON PEPPER
⅔	CUP FINE UNSEASONED BREADCRUMBS
¼	CUP SESAME SEEDS
1	EGG
1	TEASPOON MILK
4	STEAKS ¾-INCH TO 1-INCH-THICK TILEFISH (ABOUT 2 POUNDS)
2	TABLESPOONS BUTTER OR MARGARINE
2	TABLESPOONS VEGETABLE OIL
	LEMON WEDGES, PARSLEY FOR GARNISH

1 In shallow bowl or deep plate, combine flour, salt and pepper until well mixed. In another shallow bowl or deep plate, combine breadcrumbs and sesame seeds until well mixed. In third shallow bowl or deep plate, combine egg and milk until well mixed.

2 Place fish in flour mixture, then egg mixture and finally in sesame seed mixture to coat well.

3 In large nonstick skillet, heat butter and oil over medium-high heat until butter is melted. Add coated fish; cook, turning once, until golden and fish flakes easily when tested with fork, about 8 to 12 minutes.

4 Serve garnished with lemon wedges and parsley.

Herb-Coated Salmon

Serves 4

4	SMALL ¾-INCH TO 1-INCH-THICK SALMON FILLETS (ABOUT 1 POUND)
2	CLOVES GARLIC, MINCED
¼	CUP PACKED PARSLEY SPRIGS, FINELY CHOPPED
4	GREEN ONIONS, FINELY CHOPPED
2	TEASPOONS GRATED LEMON PEEL (OPTIONAL)
1	TABLESPOON OLIVE OR OTHER VEGETABLE OIL
1	TEASPOON DRIED TARRAGON
½	TEASPOON SALT
¼	TEASPOON PEPPER
2	TABLESPOONS LEMON JUICE

1 Preheat oven to 425°. Line baking sheet with foil and lightly grease. Place salmon skin side down on prepared baking sheet and set aside.

2 In small bowl, combine garlic, parsley, green onions, lemon peel, if desired, oil, tarragon, salt and pepper until well mixed. Spoon over salmon to evenly coat.

3 Bake until fish flakes easily when tested with fork, about 15 minutes. Sprinkle fish with lemon juice.

PREPARATION TIP

To prepare in the microwave, arrange salmon in a single layer in shallow microwave-safe baking dish. Cover the salmon with the herb mixture. Loosely cover with wax paper and cook on High (100% power) for 5 minutes, rotating dish once, until fish just flakes when tested with a fork.

Calories: 476 · Protein: 45 g
Fat: 24 g/ 45% Calories from Fat · Carbohydrate: 19 g
Cholesterol: 43 mg · Sodium: 678 mg

Calories: 201 · Protein: 23 g
Fat: 11 g/ 49% Calories from Fat · Carbohydrate: 2 g
Cholesterol: 62 mg · Sodium: 328 mg

Fish Curry

Serves 4

1 TABLESPOON BUTTER OR MARGARINE
1 TABLESPOON OLIVE OR OTHER VEGETABLE OIL
3 CLOVES GARLIC, MINCED
1 MEDIUM ONION, COARSELY CHOPPED
3 TABLESPOONS ALL-PURPOSE FLOUR
2 TABLESPOONS CURRY POWDER
1 CUP CHICKEN BROTH, FAT REMOVED
¼ TEASPOON PEPPER
PINCH CAYENNE PEPPER
½ CUP PACKED CILANTRO SPRIGS, MINCED (OPTIONAL)
1 POUND THICK BONELESS FIRM-FLESHED WHITE FISH, CUT INTO 1-INCH PIECES
1 PACKAGE (10 OUNCES) FROZEN CHOPPED SPINACH, THAWED, SQUEEZED DRY
¼ CUP SOUR CREAM
⅓ CUP UNSALTED DRY-ROASTED PEANUTS

1 In large skillet, heat butter and oil over medium-high heat until butter is melted. Add garlic and onion; cook, stirring, until onion is tender, about 3 minutes.

2 Stir in flour and curry powder; cook, stirring, until flour is well incorporated, about 30 seconds. Stir in broth, pepper, cayenne and 2 tablespoons cilantro, if desired. Bring to a boil, stirring constantly.

3 Add fish and spinach to curry mixture. Reduce heat to low; cover and simmer until fish flakes easily when tested with fork, about 5 minutes.

4 Add sour cream, peanuts and remaining cilantro, if desired; stir gently until well mixed.

Paella Salad

Serves 4

2 CUPS CHICKEN BROTH
2 CLOVES GARLIC, MINCED
2 TEASPOONS TURMERIC
½ TEASPOON PEPPER
1 CUP LONG-GRAIN RICE
¾ POUND MEDIUM SHRIMP, PEELED, DEVEINED
4 OUNCES UNSLICED HAM, CUT INTO ½-INCH CUBES
1 LARGE GREEN PEPPER, CUT INTO THIN STRIPS
1 MEDIUM RED PEPPER, COARSELY CHOPPED
¼ CUP CHOPPED PARSLEY (OPTIONAL)
3 TABLESPOONS OLIVE OR OTHER VEGETABLE OIL
2 TABLESPOONS LEMON JUICE
1¼ TEASPOONS GRATED LEMON PEEL (OPTIONAL)

1 In large skillet, combine broth, garlic, turmeric and pepper over medium-high heat. Bring to a boil. Add rice. Reduce heat to medium-low; cover and simmer 15 minutes.

2 Add shrimp to rice; cook until shrimp is cooked and rice is tender, about 5 minutes.

3 Remove from heat; stir in ham, green pepper, red pepper, parsley, if desired, oil, lemon juice and lemon peel, if desired. Serve warm or chilled.

PREPARATION TIP
To give the paella the traditional flavor and color, use ½ teaspoon saffron threads in place of the turmeric.

Calories: 312 · Protein: 28 g
Fat: 17 g/ 49% Calories from Fat · Carbohydrate: 14 g
Cholesterol: 63 mg · Sodium: 400 mg

Calories: 423 · Protein: 25 g
Fat: 16 g/ 34% Calories from Fat · Carbohydrate: 45 mg
Cholesterol: 121 mg · Sodium: 976 mg

Scallop-Mushroom Noodle Soup

Serves 4

4	CUPS LOW-SODIUM CHICKEN BROTH, FAT REMOVED
3	SLICES ¼-INCH-THICK FRESH GINGER, MINCED
1	TEASPOON ORIENTAL SESAME OIL
¼	TEASPOON RED PEPPER FLAKES
8	OUNCES SEA SCALLOPS, CUT INTO QUARTERS, OR BAY SCALLOPS
4	OUNCES BEAN SPROUTS
4	OUNCES SNOW PEAS, TRIMMED
4	OUNCES MUSHROOMS, THINLY SLICED
3	GREEN ONIONS, CUT INTO ½-INCH SLIVERS
8	OUNCES CHINESE (PASTA-LIKE) NOODLES, COOKED

1 In large saucepan or Dutch oven, combine broth, ginger, sesame oil and red pepper flakes over medium-high heat. Bring to a boil.

2 Add scallops, bean sprouts, snow peas and mushrooms. Reduce heat to low; cover and cook until vegetables are tender, about 1 to 2 minutes. Add green onions; cook 30 seconds.

3 Divide noodles into 4 shallow soup dishes. Top each with ¼ scallop-vegetable broth.

PREPARATION TIP
Chinese noodles are like pasta in texture and are made of wheat flour and water. Thin pastas such as spaghettini, angel hair or other very thin noodles can be substituted.

Calories: 332 · Protein: 22 g
Fat: 4 g/ 10% Calories from Fat · Carbohydrate: 51 g
Cholesterol: 19 mg · Sodium: 153 mg

Flounder with Lemon Cream

Serves 4

4	SMALL FLOUNDER FILLETS OR OTHER FIRM-FLESHED WHITE FISH (ABOUT 1¼ POUNDS)
2	TABLESPOONS BUTTER OR MARGARINE, MELTED
¼	CUP LEMON JUICE
1	TABLESPOON GRATED LEMON PEEL (OPTIONAL)
1	TEASPOON DRIED TARRAGON
½	TEASPOON SALT
½	TEASPOON PEPPER
1	TEASPOON DIJON MUSTARD
½	TEASPOON DRY MUSTARD
½	CUP HEAVY CREAM

1 Preheat broiler. Line broiler pan with foil. Place fish on prepared pan and set aside.

2 In small bowl, combine butter, 2 tablespoons lemon juice, 1 teaspoon lemon peel, if desired, ½ teaspoon tarragon, salt and pepper. Brush over fish.

3 Broil 4 inches from heat source 3 minutes. Turn; brush with additional lemon-butter.

4 Broil until fish flakes easily when tested with fork, about 4 to 6 minutes.

5 Meanwhile, in small mixer bowl with mixer, beat remaining 2 tablespoons lemon juice, 2 teaspoons lemon peel, if desired, ½ teaspoon tarragon, Dijon mustard and dry mustard until well mixed.

6 Gradually beat in cream in thin stream; beat just until soft peaks form. (Be careful not to overbeat and curdle.)

7 Serve fish topped with lemon cream.

Calories: 290 · Protein: 28 g
Fat: 19 g/ 58% Calories from Fat · Carbohydrate: 2 g
Cholesterol: 124 mg · Sodium: 499 mg

Fettuccine with Fresh Salmon

Serves 4

1	CUP REDUCED-SODIUM CHICKEN BROTH, FAT REMOVED
⅓	CUP DRY WHITE WINE
¾	POUND SKINNED, BONELESS SALMON FILLETS, CUT INTO ½-INCH-THICK SLICES
4	GREEN ONIONS, MINCED
1	MEDIUM RED PEPPER, DICED
1	TABLESPOON NO-SALT-ADDED TOMATO PASTE
1	TABLESPOON LEMON JUICE
¼	CUP SNIPPED FRESH DILL
1½	TEASPOONS CORNSTARCH
¼	CUP LIGHT SOUR CREAM
5	OUNCES FRESH FETTUCCINE, COOKED
5	OUNCES FRESH SPINACH FETTUCCINE, COOKED

1 In large skillet, combine broth and wine over high heat; bring to a boil. Reduce heat to low. Add salmon; cover and cook until salmon is opaque, about 4 minutes. Remove salmon and set aside.

2 To same skillet add green onions and pepper; simmer until pepper is tender, about 3 minutes. Add tomato paste and lemon juice until well mixed; simmer about 1 minute. Add dill. Increase heat to medium-high. Bring to a boil.

3 Meanwhile, in small bowl or cup, combine cornstarch and 1 tablespoon water until well mixed. Add to vegetable-broth mixture; cook, stirring constantly, until slightly thickened, about 1 minute. Reduce heat to low. Add salmon; cook until heated through, about 30 seconds. Remove from heat. Add sour cream until well mixed.

4 In large serving bowl, combine hot cooked fettuccines and salmon sauce; toss gently to evenly coat.

Calories: 419 · Protein: 29 g
Fat: 10 g/ 21% Calories from Fat · Carbohydrate: 50 g
Cholesterol: 111 mg · Sodium: 242 mg

Tuna-Spinach Salad

Serves 6

2	NAVEL ORANGES
2	TABLESPOONS CREAMY PEANUT BUTTER
2	TABLESPOONS REDUCED-SODIUM SOY SAUCE
2	TEASPOONS GROUND GINGER
2	TABLESPOONS CIDER VINEGAR
1	TABLESPOON ORIENTAL SESAME OIL
¼	TEASPOON PEPPER
8	CUPS LOOSELY PACKED FRESH SPINACH (ABOUT 6 OUNCES), TORN INTO BITE-SIZE PIECES
4	OUNCES MUSHROOMS, SLICED
2	MEDIUM CARROTS, THINLY SLICED
1	SMALL RED ONION, THINLY SLICED
4	OUNCES BEAN SPROUTS (ABOUT 1½ CUPS)
2	CANS (6½ OUNCES EACH) WATER-PACKED TUNA, DRAINED
¼	CUP PACKED CILANTRO (OPTIONAL)

1 Grate orange peel. Juice oranges to measure ⅔ cup. Set aside.

2 To make peanut dressing, in small bowl combine peanut butter, soy sauce and ground ginger until well mixed. Add orange juice, orange peel, vinegar, sesame oil and pepper until well mixed.

3 In large serving bowl, combine spinach, mushrooms, carrots, red onion and bean sprouts until well mixed. Top with tuna.

4 If desired, add cilantro to peanut dressing. Spoon dressing over salad.

Calories: 174 · Protein: 20 g
Fat: 6 g/ 31% Calories from Fat · Carbohydrate: 11 g
Cholesterol: 23 mg · Sodium: 454 mg

Parmesan Scallop Gratin

Serves 4

1	CUP CHICKEN BROTH, FAT REMOVED
¼	TEASPOON GROUND NUTMEG
¼	TEASPOON PEPPER
1	POUND SEA SCALLOPS
2	TABLESPOONS BUTTER OR MARGARINE
1	TABLESPOON ALL-PURPOSE FLOUR
¼	CUP HEAVY CREAM
2	TABLESPOONS GRATED PARMESAN CHEESE
1	TABLESPOON FINE, SEASONED BREADCRUMBS
	TABLESPOONS CHOPPED PARSLEY (OPTIONAL)

1 In medium saucepan, combine broth, nutmeg and pepper over medium-high heat. Bring to a boil. Add scallops; return to a boil. Reduce heat to low; cover and simmer until scallops are barely cooked, about 3 minutes. Remove scallops; reserve cooking liquid.

2 Preheat broiler.

3 In small saucepan, heat 1 tablespoon butter over medium heat until melted. Stir in flour; cook, stirring, until well incorporated, about 30 seconds. Add cream and ¼ cup reserved cooking liquid. Cook, stirring, until mixture just starts to simmer and thicken, about 2 minutes.

4 Add scallops to sauce; toss gently to evenly coat. In 1-quart gratin or shallow baking dish, place scallop-sauce mixture. Sprinkle with Parmesan and breadcrumbs; dot with remaining 1 tablespoon butter. Broil 4 inches from heat source until golden on top, about 2 to 4 minutes. Garnish with chopped parsley, if desired.

Calories: 238 · Protein: 22 g
Fat: 13 g/ 49% Calories from Fat · Carbohydrate: 6 g
Cholesterol: 76 mg · Sodium: 600 mg

Rotini with Flounder and Sun-Dried Tomato Pesto

Serves 4

½	CUP SUN-DRIED TOMATO HALVES (NOT OIL PACKED)
2	CLOVES GARLIC, PEELED
1	TABLESPOON PINE NUTS
1	TABLESPOON GRATED PARMESAN CHEESE
1	TABLESPOON OLIVE OR OTHER VEGETABLE OIL
¼	TEASPOON SALT
¼	CUP LOW-FAT (1%) MILK
¼	CUP ALL-PURPOSE FLOUR
¾	POUND BONELESS, SKINNED FLOUNDER FILLETS, CUT INTO 1-INCH PIECES
⅓	CUP REDUCED-SODIUM CHICKEN BROTH, FAT REMOVED
2	TEASPOONS LEMON JUICE
8	OUNCES ROTINI PASTA, COOKED

1 In medium saucepan, combine 1 cup water and tomatoes over medium-high heat; cook until tomatoes are slightly softened, about 3 minutes. Add garlic; cook until tomatoes are tender, about 2 minutes. In food processor or blender, place tomato-garlic mixture, pine nuts, Parmesan cheese, 1 teaspoon oil and salt; process until smooth, about 1 minute. Set aside.

2 In shallow bowl or deep plate, place milk. In another shallow bowl or deep plate, place flour. Dip fish in milk and then in flour.

3 In large nonstick skillet, heat remaining 2 teaspoons oil over medium heat until hot. Add coated fish; cook, turning once, until golden, about 2 to 3 minutes. Remove fish and keep warm.

4 To same skillet add broth and lemon juice, scraping up any brown bits, until slightly reduced, about 1 minute. Add tomato pesto until well mixed. Return fish to skillet; cook until heated through, about 1 minute.

5 In large serving bowl, place fish mixture and rotini; toss gently to evenly coat.

Calories: 400 · Protein: 27 g
Fat: 7 g/ 15% Calories from Fat · Carbohydrate: 56 g
Cholesterol: 42 mg · Sodium: 304 mg

Swordfish Piccata

*A takeoff on the classic veal or chicken piccata, this dish uses
a firm fish with excellent results.*

Serves 4

¼ CUP ALL-PURPOSE FLOUR
½ TEASPOON SALT
¼ TEASPOON PEPPER
1 POUND BONELESS ¾-INCH-THICK SWORDFISH
   STEAK, CUT INTO ½-INCH-WIDE STRIPS
2 TABLESPOONS BUTTER OR MARGARINE
2 TABLESPOONS OLIVE OR OTHER VEGETABLE OIL
3 LARGE SHALLOTS, HALVED, OR
   1 SMALL ONION, QUARTERED
2 CLOVES GARLIC, MINCED
⅓ CUP CHICKEN BROTH, FAT REMOVED
2 TABLESPOONS LEMON JUICE
¼ CUP CHOPPED FRESH OR
   1 TABLESPOON DRIED DILL
1 TABLESPOON GRATED LEMON PEEL
   (OPTIONAL)

1 In plastic or paper bag or shallow dish, com
bine flour, salt and pepper until well mixed
Add swordfish; toss to lightly coat and cove
completely. Remove fish and set aside.

2 In large nonstick skillet, heat butter and o
over medium-high heat until butter is melted.

3 Add shallots and garlic; cook, stirring occa
sionally, until shallots are translucent and jus
crisp-tender, about 3 minutes.

4 Add coated swordfish strips.

5 Cook until lightly browned, about 2 min
utes.

6 Turn; cook until lightly browned and fish i
cooked through, about 2 to 3 minutes.

7 Add broth, lemon juice, dill and lemon peel
if desired. Bring to a boil.

8 Serve fish topped with sauce.

PREPARATION TIP
Any firm-fleshed fish can be substituted like tuna, halibut or monkfish. Be
sure to be gentle when stirring during
cooking as fish is not as sturdy as
veal or chicken.

Calories: 291 · Protein: 24 g
Fat: 17 g/ 52% Calories from Fat · Carbohydrate: 9 g
Cholesterol: 60 mg · Sodium: 520 mg

Crab Louis

Serves 4

8 OUNCES SUGAR SNAP PEAS, STRINGS REMOVED

½ CUP PLAIN NONFAT YOGURT

3 TABLESPOONS CHILI SAUCE

1 TABLESPOON REDUCED-FAT MAYONNAISE

1 TABLESPOON LEMON JUICE

½ TEASPOON DRIED TARRAGON

¼ TEASPOON SALT

⅛ TEASPOON CAYENNE PEPPER

1 POUND LUMP CRABMEAT, PICKED OVER TO REMOVE CARTILAGE

5 PLUM TOMATOES, CUT INTO 1-INCH WEDGES

½ CUP DICED AVOCADO

4 CUPS WATERCRESS, TOUGH STEMS REMOVED

3 GRAPEFRUITS, PEELED AND SECTIONED

1 In small pot, combine boiling water and sugar snap peas; cook 30 seconds. Drain.

2 In large bowl, combine yogurt, chili sauce, mayonnaise, lemon juice, tarragon, salt and cayenne. Add reserved sugar snap peas, crabmeat, tomatoes and avocado; toss gently to evenly coat.

3 On large serving platter, place watercress, then grapefruit sections; top with crab mixture.

PREPARATION TIP
Before using lump crabmeat, either fresh or canned, carefully look over the meat and remove any bits of cartilage or shell that might still be there.

Calories: 284 · Protein: 29 g
Fat: 6 g/ 19% Calories from Fat · Carbohydrate: 30 g
Cholesterol: 114 mg · Sodium: 701 mg

Shrimp Caesar Salad

Serves 4

1 CUP REDUCED-SODIUM CHICKEN BROTH, FAT REMOVED

1 POUND MEDIUM SHRIMP, PEELED, DEVEINED

5 CLOVES GARLIC, PEELED

3 TABLESPOONS REDUCED-FAT MAYONNAISE

¼ CUP GRATED PARMESAN CHEESE

2 TABLESPOONS LEMON JUICE

½ TEASPOON GRATED LEMON PEEL

½ TEASPOON SALT

¼ TEASPOON PEPPER

4 OUNCES ITALIAN BREAD, HALVED HORIZONTALLY

2 CUPS CHERRY TOMATOES, HALVED

8 CUPS TORN ROMAINE OR ICEBERG LETTUCE

1 In large skillet, place broth over medium heat; bring to a boil. Reduce heat to low. Add shrimp; cover and simmer until opaque, about 4 minutes. Remove shrimp. When cool enough to handle, cut in half lengthwise.

2 Preheat broiler.

3 Return broth to a boil; add 4 cloves garlic, cook 2 minutes. Remove garlic, reserve ¼ cup cooking liquid. To make dressing, in food processor or blender, combine cooked garlic, reserved cooking liquid, mayonnaise, Parmesan cheese, lemon juice, lemon peel, salt and pepper, process until smooth, about 1 minute. Place in large bowl.

4 Broil bread 6 inches from heat source until lightly browned, about 1 minute per side. Rub bread with remaining clove garlic; cut bread into ½-inch chunks. Add garlic bread to dressing in bowl with shrimp, tomatoes and lettuce, toss gently to evenly coat.

Calories: 264 · Protein: 26 g
Fat: 7 g/ 23% Calories from Fat · Carbohydrate: 24 g
Cholesterol: 144 mg · Sodium: 807 mg

Spicy Tuna-Pasta Salad

Serves 4

⅓	CUP PLAIN NONFAT YOGURT
¼	CUP REDUCED-FAT SOUR CREAM
3	TABLESPOONS REDUCED-FAT MAYONNAISE
3	TABLESPOONS LEMON JUICE
1	TEASPOON GRATED LEMON PEEL
½	TEASPOON HOT PEPPER SAUCE
½	TEASPOON SALT
1	TEASPOON GROUND CUMIN
8	OUNCES ORZO PASTA, COOKED
2	CANS (6½ OUNCES) WATER-PACKED TUNA, DRAINED, FLAKED
1	RIB CELERY, DICED
½	CUP CHOPPED GREEN ONIONS
¼	CUP CHOPPED FRESH CILANTRO OR PARSLEY
6	CUPS MIXED TORN GREENS
4	TOMATOES, CUT INTO WEDGES
¼	CUP DICED AVOCADO

1 In large bowl, combine yogurt, sour cream, mayonnaise, lemon juice, lemon peel, hot pepper sauce, salt and cumin until well mixed. Add pasta, tuna, celery, green onions and cilantro; toss to evenly coat.

2 On serving platter or individual plates, arrange greens and tomatoes; top with tuna mixture. Sprinkle with avocado.

PREPARATION TIP
If you're watching your fat intake, be sure to check labels for fat content. Some brands have as much as 5 grams of fat in 2 ounces of water-packed solid white tuna, while others have only 1 gram of fat in 2 ounces.

Calories: 454 · Protein: 38 g
Fat: 7 g/ 13% Calories from Fat · Carbohydrate: 60 g
Cholesterol: 40 mg · Sodium: 731 mg

Cod Salad with Parsley Dressing

Serves 4

1	POUND ALL-PURPOSE POTATOES, PEELED, CUT INTO ½-INCH CUBES
¾	CUP BOTTLED CLAM JUICE
1	POUND BONELESS COD FILLETS
3	CLOVES GARLIC, PEELED
½	CUP FINELY CHOPPED FRESH PARSLEY
2	TABLESPOONS WHITE WINE VINEGAR
1	TABLESPOON OLIVE OR OTHER VEGETABLE OIL
1	TABLESPOON DIJON MUSTARD
½	TEASPOON SALT
¼	TEASPOON PEPPER
2	TABLESPOONS CAPERS, RINSED AND DRAINED
2	CUPS QUARTERED CHERRY TOMATOES
¼	CUP KALAMATA OR OTHER BRINE-CURED BLACK OLIVES, PITTED, CUT INTO SLIVERS
6	CUPS TORN ROMAINE LETTUCE

1 In large pot, combine potatoes and enough boiling water to cover over high heat; cook until potatoes are firm-tender, about 12 minutes. Drain; place in large bowl.

2 In medium skillet, place clam juice over medium heat. Bring to a simmer. Add cod; cover and cook until just opaque, about 9 to 10 minutes. Add garlic during last 2 minutes. Remove cod, reserve ½ cup cooking liquid and garlic. When cool enough, break cod into bite-size chunks.

3 To make parsley dressing, in food processor or blender, combine reserved cooking liquid, cooked garlic, parsley, vinegar, oil, mustard, salt, pepper and ¼ cup reserved cooked potatoes; process until smooth. Stir in capers.

4 To potatoes add reserved cod, tomatoes, parsley dressing and olives; toss gently to evenly coat. Serve cod mixture over bed of romaine.

Calories: 259 · Protein: 24 g
Fat: 7 g/ 24% Calories from Fat · Carbohydrate: 25 g
Cholesterol: 49 mg · Sodium: 773 mg

Tomato-Pepper Topped Fish

The tomato-pepper topping is a relish that is served with the fish and before it is combined,
the vinaigrette serves as a basting for the fish.

Serves 4

- **4** STEAKS ¾-INCH-THICK TUNA, COD OR HALIBUT (ABOUT 1 POUND)
- **4** MEDIUM PLUM TOMATOES (ABOUT ¾ POUND), COARSELY CHOPPED
- **1** SMALL RED PEPPER, COARSELY CHOPPED
- **3** GREEN ONIONS, COARSELY CHOPPED
- **¼** CUP FRESH LEAVES OR 1½ TEASPOONS DRIED BASIL
- **3** TABLESPOONS OLIVE OR OTHER VEGETABLE OIL
- **2** TABLESPOONS RED WINE OR CIDER VINEGAR
- **¼** TEASPOON SALT
- **½** TEASPOON PEPPER

1 Preheat broiler. Line broiler pan with foil and lightly grease.

2 Place fish on broiler pan and set aside.

3 To make relish, in medium bowl, combine chopped tomatoes, chopped red pepper, chopped green onions, basil, oil, vinegar, salt and pepper until evenly well mixed.

4 Into small bowl, drain excess liquid from relish; brush on fish.

5 Broil 4 inches from heat source until light brown and fish starts to feel firm to touch, about 4 minutes.

6 Turn; brush with additional liquid. Broil until fish is light brown and flakes easily when tested with a fork, about 4 minutes.

7 Serve fish topped with relish.

PREPARATION TIP

To cook in microwave, place fish in shallow microwave-safe baking dish. Brush fish with excess relish liquid; cover loosely with plastic wrap. Cook on High (100% power) for 6 minutes, rotating dish once. Let stand, covered, for 3 minutes.

Calories: 245 · Protein: 27 g
Fat: 13 g/ 47% Calories from Fat · Carbohydrate: 5 g
Cholesterol: 43 mg · Sodium: 186 mg

BEANS AND VEGETABLES

Pasta Primavera Salad

Spring vegetables and pasta are turned into a cool main-dish salad with the addition of a lemon-mustard dressing.

Serves 6

½ CUP PACKED FRESH LEAVES, MINCED, OR 2 TEASPOONS DRIED BASIL

3 TABLESPOONS OLIVE OR OTHER VEGETABLE OIL

2 TABLESPOONS LEMON JUICE

1 TABLESPOON DIJON MUSTARD

2 TEASPOONS GRATED LEMON PEEL (OPTIONAL)

¼ TEASPOON RED PEPPER FLAKES

½ TEASPOON SALT

¼ TEASPOON PEPPER

3 CLOVES GARLIC, PEELED

8 OUNCES MEDIUM EGG NOODLES

1 PACKAGE (10 OUNCES) FROZEN PEAS

1 PACKAGE (10 OUNCES) FROZEN ASPARAGUS

4 PLUM TOMATOES, COARSELY CHOPPED

3 GREEN ONIONS, COARSELY CHOPPED

2 TABLESPOONS GRATED PARMESAN CHEESE

1 In large saucepan, bring enough water to a boil to cook noodles over high heat.

2 To make dressing, in large salad bowl, combine basil, oil, lemon juice, mustard, lemon peel, if desired, red pepper flakes, salt and pepper.

3 To boiling water add garlic and noodles; cook until noodles are al dente, about 8 to 10 minutes.

4 Meanwhile, in large colander, place frozen peas and asparagus. Pour noodles and water over vegetables to drain. Run under cold water to cool; drain well. Cut asparagus into ½-inch pieces.

5 Mash or press garlic; add to dressing until well mixed. Add reserved noodles, peas, asparagus, tomatoes, green onions and Parmesan cheese; toss gently to evenly coat.

PREPARATION TIP
Frozen vegetables don't necessarily have to be cooked to be eaten. Running them under hot water to thaw is sufficient.

Calories: 274 · Protein: 11 g
Fat: 9 g/ 29% Calories from Fat · Carbohydrate: 38 g
Cholesterol: 37 mg · Sodium: 357 mg

Pesto with Linguine

Serves 6

2½ CUPS LOOSELY PACKED FRESH BASIL LEAVES
2 CLOVES GARLIC
⅓ CUP PINE NUTS OR WALNUTS, TOASTED
¾ CUP GRATED PARMESAN CHEESE
½ CUP OLIVE OIL
SALT AND PEPPER TO TASTE
¾ POUND LINGUINE

1 To make pesto in food processor or blender, place basil, garlic, pine nuts and ½ cup Parmesan cheese; process until well combined. With machine on, gradually add oil. Add salt and pepper to taste.

2 Cook linguine according to package directions. Drain, reserving 2 tablespoons cooking liquid.

3 In large serving bowl, combine hot linguine, pesto and reserved cooking liquid; toss to evenly coat. Serve immediately with remaining ¼ cup Parmesan cheese.

PREPARATION TIP
While fresh basil is the classic for pesto, half basil and half of another green such as mild spinach or for a spicy pesto half mache, watercress or arugula can be used.

Calories: 451 · Protein: 13 g
Fat: 26 g/ 51% Calories from Fat · Carbohydrate: 43 g
Cholesterol: 7 mg · Sodium: 194 mg

Tomato-Vegetable Soup with Pesto

Serves 4

1 TABLESPOON OLIVE OR OTHER VEGETABLE OIL
1 LARGE ONION, CHOPPED
1 MEDIUM ZUCCHINI, HALVED LENGTHWISE AND SLICED
1 MEDIUM YELLOW SQUASH, HALVED LENGTHWISE AND SLICED
1 CLOVE GARLIC, MINCED
3½ CUPS VEGETABLE BROTH
1 CAN (16 OUNCES) NO-SALT-ADDED WHOLE TOMATOES, DRAINED, CHOPPED
1 CAN (19 OUNCES) WHITE KIDNEY BEANS (CANNELLONI), DRAINED AND RINSED
2 TABLESPOONS PESTO
GRATED ROMANO CHEESE FOR GARNISH

1 In large saucepan, heat oil over medium heat until hot. Add onion; cook until soft, about 5 minutes. Add zucchini, yellow squash and garlic; cook, stirring occasionally, until squash is crisp-tender, about 5 minutes.

2 Add vegetable broth, tomatoes, beans and pesto; cook 10 minutes.

3 Serve with Romano cheese, if desired.

PREPARATION TIP
Pesto (see recipe at left) can be made ahead and stored tightly covered in the refrigerator for several weeks. It can also be found ready-to-use in the refrigerator section of a supermarket, usually next to the fresh pasta and dairy foods.

Calories: 233 · Protein: 10 g
Fat: 8 g/ 32% Calories from Fat · Carbohydrate: 31 g
Cholesterol: 0 mg · Sodium: 480 mg

Asian-Style Tofu and Vegetables

*Here the protein components, tofu and cannellini beans, just need to be heated through,
thus cutting the cooking time down to close to nothing.*

Serves 4

2½	CUPS WATER
1	CUP LONG-GRAIN RICE
¼	TEASPOON SALT
2	TEASPOONS VEGETABLE OIL
4	GREEN ONIONS, THINLY SLICED
2	CLOVES GARLIC, MINCED
1	RED PEPPER, CUT INTO ½-INCH PIECES
⅓	CUP ORANGE JUICE
¼	CUP CHILI SAUCE
2	TABLESPOONS PLUM JAM
2	TABLESPOONS REDUCED-SODIUM SOY SAUCE
¾	TEASPOON GROUND GINGER
8	OUNCES SNOW PEAS, HALVED CROSSWISE
½	CUP SLICED WATER CHESTNUTS
1	CAN (19 OUNCES) WHITE KIDNEY BEANS (CANNELLONI), RINSED AND DRAINED
8	OUNCES FIRM TOFU, CUT INTO ½-INCH CUBES

1 In medium saucepan, place water over high heat. Bring to a boil; add rice and salt. Reduce heat to low; cover and simmer until rice is tender, about 17 minutes.

2 Meanwhile, in large skillet, heat oil over medium heat until hot. Add green onions and garlic; cook, stirring frequently, until green onions are tender, about 2 minutes. Add pepper; cook until crisp-tender, about 2 minutes.

3 In small bowl, combine orange juice, chili sauce, plum jam, soy sauce and ginger until well mixed.

4 Add to skillet with snow peas and water chestnuts. Bring to a boil.

5 Add kidney beans; cook just until heated through, about 2 minutes.

6 Add tofu; cook, stirring gently, until heated through, about 3 minutes.

7 Serve with rice.

PREPARATION TIP
To trim fresh snow peas, snip off stem end and pull off the string along the straight side.

Calories: 470 · Protein: 23 g
Fat: 9 g/ 17% Calories from Fat · Carbohydrate: 78 g
Cholesterol: 0 mg · Sodium: 853 mg

Lemony Spinach-Rice Soup

A takeoff of the delicious Greek soup called Avgolemono made with eggs and lemon juice, this soup is a little more substantial with the addition of rice and spinach.

Serves 6

6 CUPS CHICKEN BROTH, FAT REMOVED
1 CUP WATER
⅔ CUP LONG-GRAIN RICE
½ TEASPOON PEPPER
2 EGGS, LIGHTLY BEATEN
½ POUND FRESH SPINACH, TRIMMED, TORN INTO BITE-SIZE PIECES
6 TABLESPOONS LEMON JUICE

1 In medium saucepan, combine broth and water over medium-high heat. Bring to a boil.

2 Add rice and pepper. Reduce heat to medium-low; cover and simmer until rice is almost tender, about 15 minutes.

3 In small bowl, combine ¼ cup hot broth and eggs; beat until well mixed. Slowly pour into remaining hot broth-rice mixture.

4 Slowly pour broth-egg mixture into remaining hot broth-rice mixture.

5 Add spinach and lemon juice. Reduce heat to low; cook, stirring constantly, until egg is cooked and rice is tender, about 5 to 8 minutes. (Do not allow to simmer or egg will curdle.)

PREPARATION TIP
For less preparation and to save time, use 1 package (10 ounces) frozen chopped spinach that has been thawed and squeezed dry instead of fresh spinach.

Calories: 137 · Protein: 7 g
Fat: 3 g/ 19% Calories from Fat · Carbohydrate: 20 g
Cholesterol: 71 mg · Sodium: 1,033 mg

Penne with Pepper, White Beans and Thyme

A vegetarian delight of pasta and beans, "pasta e fagioli" in Italian, that combines protein-rich white beans with pasta enhanced by colorful peppers.

Serves 6

3	TABLESPOONS OLIVE OR OTHER VEGETABLE OIL
1	MEDIUM RED ONION, THINLY SLICED
3	CLOVES GARLIC, MINCED
1	LARGE GREEN PEPPER, CUT INTO BITE-SIZE PIECES
1	LARGE YELLOW PEPPER, CUT INTO BITE-SIZE PIECES
8	OUNCES PENNE OR OTHER MEDIUM-LARGE TUBE PASTA
1	CAN (16 OUNCES) SMALL WHITE BEANS, RINSED AND DRAINED
2	TABLESPOONS LEMON JUICE
1	TEASPOON DRIED THYME
¾	TEASPOON SALT
¼	TEASPOON PEPPER
2	TABLESPOONS BUTTER OR MARGARINE

1 In large skillet, heat 2 tablespoons oil ove medium-high heat until hot.

2 Add onion and garlic; cook until onion be gins to brown and is just crisp-tender, about ! minutes.

3 To same skillet add remaining 1 tablespoo oil. Add green and yellow peppers; cook, stirrin; frequently, until peppers are just crisp-tender about 5 to 8 minutes.

4 Cook pasta according to package directions

5 Add beans, lemon juice, thyme, salt an(pepper; cook until beans are heated through about 3 minutes.

6 Drain pasta; place hot pasta in large shallov serving bowl.

7 Add butter; toss until evenly coated.

8 To hot buttered pasta add pepper-bea mixture; toss gently to evenly coat.

NOTE: If desired other beans, red or whit kidney, pink or black beans can be substituted

---

PREPARATION TIP
To cut down on fat and calories, omit the butter or just use one tablespoon instead of two.

Calories: 339 · Protein: 11 g
Fat: 12 g/ 31% Calories from Fat · Carbohydrate: 49 g
Cholesterol: 10 mg · Sodium: 323 mg

Linguine and Broccoli with Peanut Sauce

Serves 6

½ CUP PLUS 2 TABLESPOONS CREAMY PEANUT BUTTER
¼ CUP REDUCED-SODIUM SOY SAUCE
2 TABLESPOONS ORIENTAL SESAME OIL
2 TEASPOONS WHITE VINEGAR
½ CUP CHICKEN BROTH, FAT REMOVED
8 OUNCES LINGUINE OR SPAGHETTI
3 TABLESPOONS VEGETABLE OIL
3 CLOVES GARLIC, MINCED
2 STALKS BROCCOLI, CUT INTO BITE-SIZE PIECES
1 LARGE RED PEPPER, CUT INTO BITE-SIZE PIECES
6 TO 8 GREEN ONIONS, COARSELY CHOPPED
½ CUP PACKED CILANTRO (OPTIONAL)

1 To make peanut sauce, in food processor or blender, combine peanut butter, soy sauce, sesame oil and vinegar; process until smooth. With machine on, gradually add broth until smooth. Set aside.

2 In large saucepan, cook linguine according to package directions.

3 In large skillet, heat oil over medium-high heat until hot. Add garlic; cook 1 minute. Add broccoli and pepper; cook, stirring constantly, until vegetables are just tender, about 5 to 8 minutes. Add green onions and cilantro, if desired.

4 Drain linguine; place in large serving bowl. Add vegetables and peanut sauce; toss gently to evenly coat.

Apple-Butternut Soup

Serves 4

2 TABLESPOONS BUTTER OR MARGARINE
1 MEDIUM ONION, THICKLY SLICED
2½ CUPS CHICKEN BROTH
1 SMALL BUTTERNUT SQUASH (ABOUT 1 POUND), PEELED, CUT INTO LARGE CUBES
5 SMALL WHITE POTATOES (ABOUT ½ POUND), HALVED
¼ TEASPOON SALT
¼ TEASPOON PEPPER
1½ CUPS UNSWEETENED APPLESAUCE

1 In medium saucepan, heat butter over medium heat until melted. Add onion; cook until tender, about 7 minutes.

2 Add broth, squash, potatoes, salt and pepper. Increase heat to medium-high. Bring to a boil. Reduce heat to medium-low; cover and simmer until potatoes and squash are tender, about 15 minutes.

3 In food processor or blender, place cooked vegetables; process until smooth. Add applesauce; process until well mixed. Return puréed vegetable-applesauce mixture to broth.

4 Cook until heated through.

> **PREPARATION TIP**
> In place of applesauce, 4 medium-size apples (delicious, golden delicious, gala, etc.), peeled and cut into chunks can be used in Step 3.

Calories: 410 · Protein: 15 g
Fat: 24 g/ 52% Calories from Fat · Carbohydrate: 38 g
Cholesterol: 0 mg · Sodium: 623 mg

Calories: 199 · Protein: 4 g
Fat: 7 g/ 31% Calories from Fat · Carbohydrate: 33 g
Cholesterol: 16 mg · Sodium: 820 mg

Light Mushroom and Pepper Frittata

This Italian omelet is lightened by using three whole eggs plus two egg whites
in place of the six to eight whole eggs normally used.

Serves 4

¼	CUP CHICKEN BROTH, FAT REMOVED
1	TEASPOON DRIED THYME
1	LARGE RED PEPPER, CUT INTO THIN STRIPS
6	TO 8 GREEN ONIONS, COARSELY CHOPPED
4	OUNCES SMALL MUSHROOMS, HALVED
3	WHOLE EGGS PLUS 2 EGG WHITES
¼	TEASPOON SALT
¼	TEASPOON PEPPER
1	TABLESPOON BUTTER OR MARGARINE

1 In medium saucepan, combine broth and ½ teaspoon thyme over medium-high heat. Bring to a boil. Add red pepper, green onions and mushrooms. Reduce heat to medium-low; cover and simmer, stirring occasionally, until pepper is crisp-tender, about 5 minutes.

2 Uncover; increase heat to medium. Boil off any remaining liquid, about 3 to 5 minutes.

3 Meanwhile, in medium bowl, combine remaining ½ teaspoon thyme, whole eggs, egg whites, salt and pepper until well mixed.

4 Preheat broiler.

5 In medium ovenproof skillet, heat butter over medium-high heat until melted. Add cooked vegetables and egg mixture to evenly distribute. Reduce heat to medium; cover and cook until almost set, about 7 to 10 minutes. Broil 4 inches from heat source until completely set and top is brown, about 5 minutes.

PREPARATION TIP
Anything goes into a frittata; so it's a great way to use leftover bits of meat, chicken, seafood, cheese and vegetables and turn them into a hearty meal.

Calories: 120 · Protein: 9 g
Fat: 7 g/ 52% Calories from Fat · Carbohydrate: 6 g
Cholesterol: 159 mg · Sodium: 309 mg

Radiatore Alla Norma

Cooked in a flavorful sauce of balsamic vinegar, the eggplant in this dish becomes meat-like in texture and very satisfying.

Serves 4

2	TABLESPOONS OLIVE OR OTHER VEGETABLE OIL
1	LARGE ONION, FINELY CHOPPED
3	CLOVES GARLIC, MINCED
1	POUND EGGPLANT, CUT INTO ½-INCH-WIDE STRIPS
¼	CUP BALSAMIC VINEGAR
1	TABLESPOON SUGAR
2	CUPS CANNED CRUSHED TOMATOES
2	TABLESPOONS CHOPPED FRESH OR ½ TEASPOON DRIED BASIL
½	TEASPOON SALT
¼	TEASPOON PEPPER
12	OUNCES RADIATORE PASTA, COOKED
½	CUP PART-SKIM RICOTTA CHEESE

1 In large nonstick skillet, heat oil over medium heat until hot. Add onion and garlic; cook, stirring frequently, until onion is soft, about 7 minutes.

2 Add eggplant, vinegar, sugar and ½ cup water. Bring to a boil. Reduce heat to low; cover and simmer until eggplant is tender, about 7 minutes.

3 Add tomato; cook, stirring frequently, until slightly thickened, about 5 minutes. Remove from heat. Add basil, salt and pepper.

4 In large serving bowl, combine cooked radiatore and eggplant-tomato mixture; toss gently to evenly coat. Serve topped with a dollop of ricotta cheese.

Calories: 505 · Protein: 17 g
Fat: 11 g/ 19% Calories from Fat · Carbohydrate: 86 g
Cholesterol: 10 mg · Sodium: 521 mg

Noodles and Mushrooms with Creamy Poppy-Seed Sauce

This dish of noodles tossed with sautéed onions, mushrooms,
a sour cream-yogurt sauce and poppy seeds has its roots in German and eastern European cooking.

Serves 4

2	TABLESPOONS OLIVE OR OTHER VEGETABLE OIL
2	MEDIUM ONIONS, THINLY SLICED
2	CLOVES GARLIC, MINCED
2	TABLESPOONS BUTTER OR MARGARINE
8	OUNCES MUSHROOMS, THINLY SLICED
⅓	CUP LEMON JUICE
¾	TEASPOON SALT
½	TEASPOON PEPPER
	PINCH CAYENNE PEPPER
¾	POUND MEDIUM EGG NOODLES
⅓	CUP SOUR CREAM
⅓	CUP PLAIN YOGURT
2	TABLESPOONS POPPY SEEDS
1	TABLESPOON GRATED LEMON PEEL (OPTIONAL)

1 In medium skillet, heat oil over medium-high heat until hot. Add onions and garlic; cook until onions begin to brown, about 5 minutes.

2 To same skillet add butter and mushrooms; cook until mushrooms begin to soften, about 5 minutes. Add lemon juice, salt and peppers. Bring to a boil. Reduce heat to low; cover and simmer 4 to 6 minutes.

3 In large saucepan, cook noodles according to package directions.

4 In small bowl, combine sour cream, yogurt, poppy seeds and lemon peel, if desired. Drain noodles.

5 In large serving bowl, combine hot noodles, mushroom mixture and sour cream mixture; toss gently until well coated.

PREPARATION TIP
To bring out the nut-like taste of poppy seeds, place them in a hot ungreased skillet over medium-high heat for a few seconds until toasted.

Calories: 546 · Protein: 16g
Fat: 23 g/ 37% Calories from Fat · Carbohydrate: 71 g
Cholesterol: 106 mg · Sodium: 520 mg

Modern Minestrone

Serves 6

3½ CUPS BEEF BROTH, FAT REMOVED
1½ CUPS WATER
1 CAN (16 OUNCES) CRUSHED TOMATOES
1 TEASPOON DRIED BASIL
¼ TEASPOON PEPPER
1 CAN (15 OUNCES) BLACK BEANS,
RINSED AND DRAINED
1 MEDIUM ONION, COARSELY CHOPPED
1 LARGE CARROT, COARSELY CHOPPED
3 CLOVES GARLIC, MINCED
1 CUP FROZEN PEAS
1 CUP ELBOW MACARONI
⅓ CUP GRATED PARMESAN CHEESE

1 In 4-quart saucepan, combine broth, water, tomatoes, basil and pepper over high heat. Bring to a boil.

2 Add beans, onion, carrot, garlic, peas and macaroni. Reduce heat to medium-low; cover and simmer, stirring occasionally, until macaroni is al dente, about 12 minutes.

3 Serve with Parmesan cheese.

PREPARATION TIP
To turn this easy, hearty soup into vegetarian fare, substitute vegetable broth for beef broth and if desired omit the Parmesan cheese.

Calories: 226 · Protein: 13 g
Fat: 3 g/ 11% Calories from Fat · Carbohydrate: 37 g
Cholesterol: 4 mg · Sodium: 922 mg

Potato Cakes

Serves 6

½ CUP SOUR CREAM
½ CUP FINELY CHOPPED GREEN ONIONS
½ TEASPOON PEPPER
2 POUNDS ALL-PURPOSE POTATOES, PEELED
2 LARGE EGGS, LIGHTLY BEATEN
¼ CUP ALL-PURPOSE FLOUR
2 CLOVES GARLIC, MINCED
½ TEASPOON SALT
2 TO 3 TABLESPOONS OLIVE OR
OTHER VEGETABLE OIL

1 In small bowl, combine sour cream, green onions and ¼ teaspoon pepper until well mixed. Cover and refrigerate.

2 Preheat oven to 300°.

3 Over large bowl, grate or shred potatoes. Add remaining ¼ teaspoon pepper, eggs, flour, garlic and salt until well mixed.

4 In large heavy skillet, heat 1 tablespoon oil over medium heat until hot. Add ¼ cup potato mixture in mounds and flatten into cakes.

5 Cook until edges are crisp and browned, about 3 to 4 minutes.

6 Turn; cook until golden brown, about 3 to 4 minutes. Transfer to ovenproof platter and keep warm, uncovered, in preheated oven.

7 Repeat with remaining potato mixture, adding more oil as needed.

8 Serve with green onion-sour cream mixture.

Calories: 291· Protein: 6 g
Fat: 11 g/ 36% Calories from Fat · Carbohydrate: 41 g
Cholesterol: 100 mg · Sodium: 222 mg

Spinach Pasta with Cauliflower-Cheddar Sauce

It's the flavor of sharp Cheddar cheese that gives this dish its richness and full taste.
Select a variety from the states of New York, Wisconsin or Vermont.

Serves 8

12 OUNCES SPINACH FETTUCCINE

1 SMALL HEAD CAULIFLOWER
   (ABOUT 1¾ POUNDS),
   CUT INTO BITE-SIZE PIECES

4 TABLESPOONS BUTTER OR MARGARINE

2 CLOVES GARLIC, MINCED

⅓ CUP ALL-PURPOSE FLOUR

½ CUP CHICKEN BROTH, FAT REMOVED

1 CUP MILK

8 OUNCES SHARP CHEDDAR CHEESE,
   SHREDDED (ABOUT 2 CUPS)

3 TABLESPOONS DIJON MUSTARD

¼ TEASPOON PEPPER

1 In large pot, combine boiling water and fettuccine over high heat. Cook until al dente, about 10 to 12 minutes. Add cauliflower during last 5 minutes.

2 Meanwhile, in medium saucepan, heat butter over medium heat until melted. Add garlic; cook 1 minute. Add flour; cook, stirring constantly, until flour is incorporated, about 30 seconds. Slowly add broth, stirring constantly, until smooth.

3 Add milk, Cheddar cheese, mustard and pepper; cook, stirring occasionally, until cheese is melted.

4 Drain pasta and cauliflower; place in large serving bowl. Add Cheddar sauce; toss gently to evenly coat.

PREPARATION TIP

To make the sauce in the microwave, place the butter and garlic in a 4-cup glass measure. Cook on High (100% power) for 1 minute or until butter melts. Stir in the flour, then gradually add broth. Stir in milk, mustard and pepper. Cook on High for 3 minutes or until hot. Stir in Cheddar; cook on Medium (50% power) for 3 minutes or until cheese is melted, stirring once.

Calories: 384 · Protein: 16 g
Fat: 19 g/ 44% Calories from Fat · Carbohydrate: 39 g
Cholesterol: 90 mg · Sodium: 516 mg

Fettuccine with Green Vegetables

Serves 6

8 OUNCES FETTUCCINE OR OTHER WIDE NOODLES

3 TABLESPOONS BUTTER OR MARGARINE

3 TABLESPOONS OLIVE OR OTHER VEGETABLE OIL

6 TO 8 GREEN ONIONS, COARSELY CHOPPED

5 CLOVES GARLIC, MINCED

1 PACKAGE (10 OUNCES) FROZEN CHOPPED SPINACH, THAWED, SQUEEZED DRY

1 CUP FROZEN PEAS, THAWED

1 CUP FROZEN CHOPPED BROCCOLI, THAWED

¾ TEASPOON SALT

½ TEASPOON PEPPER

1¼ CUPS SOUR CREAM

⅔ CUP GRATED PARMESAN CHEESE

1 In large saucepan, cook fettuccine according to package directions.

2 In large skillet, heat butter and oil over medium heat until butter is melted. Add green onions and garlic; cook until green onions are limp, about 5 minutes.

3 Increase heat to medium-high. Add spinach, peas, broccoli, salt and pepper. Cook, stirring, until vegetables are heated through, about 5 minutes.

4 Stir in sour cream and remove from heat.

5 Drain fettuccine; place in large serving bowl. Add vegetable mixture and Parmesan cheese; toss gently to evenly coat.

South-of-the-Border Black Bean Soup

Serves 6

1 TABLESPOON VEGETABLE OIL

1 MEDIUM ONION, COARSELY CHOPPED

2 CLOVES GARLIC, MINCED

2¾ CUPS VEGETABLE BROTH

2 CANS (16 OUNCES EACH) BLACK BEANS, RINSED AND DRAINED

1 PACKAGE (10 OUNCES) FROZEN WHOLE-KERNEL CORN, THAWED

1 TABLESPOON CHILI POWDER

1½ TEASPOONS DRIED OREGANO

PINCH CAYENNE PEPPER

1 BAY LEAF

¼ CUP CHOPPED CILANTRO (OPTIONAL)

½ CUP SOUR CREAM (OPTIONAL)

1 In large saucepan, heat oil over medium high heat until hot. Add onion and garlic cook until onion begins to brown, about minutes.

2 Add broth, black beans, corn, chili powder oregano, cayenne and bay leaf. Bring to a boil Reduce heat to medium-low; cover and simmer 15 minutes. Remove bay leaf.

3 With slotted spoon, remove about 1½ cup vegetables; place in food processor or blender Process until smooth. Return purée to soup.

4 Cook until heated through. Serve sprinkle with cilantro and topped with sour cream, desired.

Calories: 440 · Protein: 14 g
Fat: 27 g/ 55% Calories from Fat · Carbohydrate: 37 g
Cholesterol: 80 mg · Sodium: 599 mg

Calories: 237 · Protein: 13g
Fat: 4 g/ 15% Calories from Fat · Carbohydrate: 40 g
Cholesterol: 0 mg · Sodium: 835 mg

Vegetable Antipasto Salad

Antipasto is generally little tidbits eaten before the main meal in Italian cuisine.
Here with the addition of cheese it is turned into a filling main dish.

erves 4

- CUP REDUCED-SODIUM CHICKEN BROTH, FAT REMOVED
- CUP BALSAMIC VINEGAR
- TABLESPOON OLIVE OR OTHER VEGETABLE OIL
- TEASPOON FIRMLY PACKED LIGHT BROWN SUGAR
- TEASPOON DRIED OREGANO
- TEASPOON SALT
- TEASPOON PEPPER
- POUND ALL-PURPOSE POTATOES
- PACKAGES (9 OUNCES EACH) FROZEN ARTICHOKE HEARTS
- CAN (19 OUNCES) RED KIDNEY BEANS, RINSED AND DRAINED
- RIBS CELERY, THINLY SLICED
- RED PEPPER, CUT INTO ½-INCH PIECES
- YELLOW PEPPER, CUT INTO ½-INCH PIECES
- OUNCES PROVOLONE CHEESE, CUT INTO ¼-INCH CUBES

1 To make dressing, in large bowl, combine broth, vinegar, oil, brown sugar, oregano, salt and pepper until well combined.

2 In large pot, combine boiling water and potatoes over medium-high heat; cook until potatoes are tender, about 25 minutes.

3 When potatoes are cool enough to handle, peel and cut into ½-inch cubes. Add potatoes to dressing.

4 Meanwhile, cook artichoke hearts according to package directions. Drain well; add to potato-dressing mixture.

5 Add beans, celery and peppers; toss until evenly coated. Cover and refrigerate at least 1 hour or up to 8 hours.

6 Just before serving, add provolone cheese; toss gently to evenly coat.

PREPARATION TIP
This is a great picnic dish. Complete the meal with crusty Italian bread and fresh fruit for dessert.

Calories: 386 · Protein: 20 g
Fat: 12 g/ 27% Calories from Fat · Carbohydrate: 52 g
Cholesterol: 20 mg · Sodium: 705 mg

Calabacitas

Serves 4

1 TABLESPOON OLIVE OIL
4 TABLESPOONS BUTTER OR MARGARINE
4 MEDIUM ZUCCHINI, HALVED LENGTHWISE, CUT INTO ½-INCH SLICES
1 MEDIUM ONION, CHOPPED
1 MEDIUM RED PEPPER, CUT INTO THIN STRIPS
1 JALAPEÑO PEPPER, SEEDED AND MINCED
2 CLOVES GARLIC, MINCED
1 CUP WHOLE-KERNEL CORN
½ CUP HEAVY CREAM
½ TEASPOON SALT
¼ TEASPOON PEPPER
2 OUNCES CHEDDAR CHEESE, SHREDDED (½ CUP)

1 In large skillet, heat oil and butter over medium-high heat until butter is melted. Add zucchini, onion, red pepper, jalapeño and garlic; cook, stirring occasionally, until zucchini is soft, about 5 minutes.

2 Add corn, cream, salt and pepper. Reduce heat to low; cover and simmer until zucchini is crisp-tender, about 5 minutes.

3 Remove from heat. Add Cheddar; stir until cheese is just melted. Serve immediately.

PREPARATION TIP
If desired, canned chopped jalapeño peppers, whichever you prefer mild or hot, can be substituted for the fresh jalapeño pepper.

Calories: 399 · Protein: 10 g
Fat: 31 g/ 67% Calories from Fat · Carbohydrate: 24 g
Cholesterol: 86 mg · Sodium: 474 mg

Broccoli and Ricotta Pizza

Serves 4

1 FULLY BAKED ITALIAN FLATBREAD SHELL (ABOUT 1 POUND)
1 CUP PART-SKIM RICOTTA CHEESE
1 PACKAGE (10 OUNCES) FROZEN CHOPPED BROCCOLI, COOKED
¼ TEASPOON SALT
¼ TEASPOON PEPPER
4 OUNCES MOZZARELLA CHEESE, SHREDDED (4 OUNCES)
1 TEASPOON RED PEPPER FLAKES (OPTIONAL)

1 Preheat oven to 450°. Place flatbread shell on baking sheet. Spread evenly with ricotta cheese to within 1 inch of edge.

2 Top evenly with broccoli; sprinkle with salt and pepper, then the mozzarella cheese.

3 Bake until edge of crust is browned and cheese is bubbly, about 10 to 12 minutes.

4 Sprinkle with red pepper flakes, if desired.

PREPARATION TIP
For other variations try thawed frozen, squeezed dry chopped spinach, cut green beans or asparagus, cut into 2-inch pieces in place of the broccoli.

Calories: 498 · Protein: 25 g
Fat: 12 g/ 21% Calories from Fat · Carbohydrate: 71 g
Cholesterol: 40 mg · Sodium: 998 mg

Curried Zucchini Soup

Sparked with garlic, basil and curry powder,
this puréed soup is enriched with sour cream and yogurt for a full flavor.

erves 4

CUPS LOW-SODIUM CHICKEN BROTH,
FAT REMOVED

CLOVES GARLIC, MINCED

TABLESPOONS CURRY POWDER

TEASPOON PEPPER

LARGE ZUCCHINI (ABOUT 1 POUND),
CUT INTO 1-INCH PIECES

GREEN ONIONS, COARSELY CHOPPED

TABLESPOONS CHOPPED FRESH OR
1½ TEASPOONS DRIED BASIL

TABLESPOONS PLAIN YOGURT

TABLESPOONS SOUR CREAM

TABLESPOONS CORNSTARCH

1 In medium saucepan, combine broth, garlic, curry powder and pepper over medium-high heat. Bring to a boil.

2 Add zucchini, green onions and basil. Reduce heat to low; cover and simmer until zucchini is tender, about 10 minutes.

3 In food processor or blender, place cooked vegetables; process until smooth.

4 In large bowl, combine 4 tablespoons yogurt, sour cream and cornstarch. Add puréed vegetable mixture until well mixed.

5 Add vegetable-yogurt mixture to broth. Increase heat to medium; bring to a boil. Cook, stirring, until slightly thickened, about 1 to 2 minutes.

6 Serve with remaining 2 tablespoons yogurt.

PREPARATION TIP
Try this same technique with other vegetables such as cooked butternut or acorn squash or sweet potatoes.

Calories: 107 · Protein: 5 g
Fat: 4 g/ 33% Calories from Fat · Carbohydrate: 15 g
Cholesterol: 4 mg · Sodium: 66 mg

Two-Bean Salad

Serves 6

⅓   CUP OLIVE OR OTHER VEGETABLE OIL
¼   CUP RED WINE OR CIDER VINEGAR
2   TABLESPOONS GRAINY OR
     REGULAR DIJON MUSTARD
1   CLOVE GARLIC, MINCED
2   TABLESPOONS CHOPPED PARSLEY (OPTIONAL)
1   TEASPOON DRIED TARRAGON
¼   TEASPOON DRY MUSTARD
½   TEASPOON SALT
¼   TEASPOON PEPPER
8   OUNCES MUSHROOMS, SLICED
1   PACKAGE (10 OUNCES) FROZEN GREEN BEANS,
     THAWED
1   CAN (15¼ OUNCES) RED KIDNEY BEANS,
     RINSED AND DRAINED
8   OUNCES GRUYÈRE, EMMENTHALER,
     JARLSBERG OR SWISS CHEESE, SHREDDED
1   CUP PECAN HALVES, TOASTED

1 To make dressing, in large salad bowl, combine oil, vinegar, Dijon mustard, garlic, parsley, if desired, tarragon, dry mustard, salt and pepper until well mixed.

2 Add mushrooms; toss to evenly coat. Add green beans, kidney beans and cheese; toss to evenly coat.

3 Just before serving, add pecans; toss until well mixed.

Greek Green Bean Salad

Serves 4

1   POUND FRESH GREEN BEANS,
     CUT INTO 2-INCH PIECES
3   TABLESPOONS OLIVE OR OTHER VEGETABLE OIL
3   TABLESPOONS RED WINE OR CIDER VINEGAR
1   CLOVE GARLIC, MINCED
1½   TEASPOONS DRIED OREGANO
¼   TEASPOON PEPPER
1   SMALL RED ONION, HALVED, THINLY SLICED
½   CUP OIL-CURED BLACK OLIVES
4   OUNCES FETA CHEESE, CRUMBLED
     (ABOUT 1 CUP)

1 In large saucepan over medium-high heat, place green beans in steamer basket over boiling water; cook until crisp-tender, about 8 minutes. Run under cold water; drain and set aside.

2 To make dressing, in small bowl, combine oil, vinegar, garlic, oregano and pepper.

3 In large salad bowl, combine reserved green beans, dressing, onion and olives; toss until evenly coated. Top with crumbled feta cheese.

PREPARATION TIP
To toast the pecans in the microwave, place them in a shallow microwave-safe bowl or glass pie plate, and drizzle with 1 teaspoon of oil. Cook on High (100% power) for 3 to 4 minutes, stirring once about halfway through.

PREPARATION TIP
For a fuller, richer more authentic flavor, use extra-virgin olive oil and oil-cured Greek black olives, both available at large supermarkets.

Calories: 465 · Protein: 18 g
Fat: 37 g/ 71% Calories from Fat · Carbohydrate: 18 g
Cholesterol: 42 mg · Sodium: 552 mg

Calories: 219· Protein: 6 g
Fat: 17 g/ 67% Calories from Fat · Carbohydrate: 12 g
Cholesterol: 25 mg · Sodium: 346 mg

Bean Burritos

*Serve these hearty meatless burritos topped with sour cream and salsa
with avocado slices or guacamole on the side.*

Serves 4

2	TABLESPOONS OLIVE OR OTHER VEGETABLE OIL
1	MEDIUM ONION, CHOPPED
2	CLOVES GARLIC, MINCED
1	JALAPEÑO PEPPER, SEEDED AND MINCED
1	CAN (16 OUNCES) PINTO, BLACK OR PINK BEANS, RINSED AND DRAINED
1	TEASPOON CUMIN
½	TEASPOON SALT
¼	TEASPOON PEPPER
¼	CUP CHOPPED CILANTRO
8	FLOUR TORTILLAS (7-INCH DIAMETER)
4	GREEN ONIONS, CHOPPED
3	OUNCES MONTEREY JACK CHEESE, SHREDDED (3 OUNCES)

1 In large skillet, heat oil over medium-low heat until hot. Add onion, garlic and jalapeño; cook, stirring, until onion is tender, about 5 minutes.

2 Add beans and 3 tablespoons water. Cook, stirring and mashing with back of spoon until coarse purée. Add cumin.

3 Increase heat to medium-high; cook, stirring, until thickened, about 5 minutes. Add salt, pepper and cilantro.

4 Preheat oven to 300°. Grease shallow baking dish; set aside.

5 Wrap tortillas in a large piece of foil; bake until warm and soft, about 5 to 8 minutes.

6 Working quickly, down center of each tortilla place ⅛ bean mixture; top with ⅛ green onions and cheese.

7 Roll up; place seam side down in single layer in prepared pan.

8 Bake until cheese melts, about 5 to 8 minutes.

PREPARATION TIP
Many varieties of beans can be used in this recipe. Or, try substituting shredded chicken or turkey for all or part of the beans.

Calories: 499 · Protein: 20 g
Fat: 18 g/ 32% Calories from Fat · Carbohydrate: 67 g
Cholesterol: 19 mg · Sodium: 619 mg

Spanish Omelet

This light, easy to make omelet can be filled with a wide variety of fillings and other combinations.

Serves 4

2	TABLESPOONS VEGETABLE OIL
1	MEDIUM ONION, DICED
1	MEDIUM GREEN PEPPER, DICED
1	MEDIUM TOMATO, SEEDED AND DICED
2	CLOVES GARLIC, MINCED
½	TEASPOON SALT
¼	TEASPOON RED PEPPER FLAKES
12	LARGE EGGS
¼	CUP CHOPPED FRESH HERBS (OREGANO, BASIL, CHIVES, ETC.)
4	TABLESPOONS BUTTER OR MARGARINE

PREPARATION TIP

To serve all at the same time, place completed omelet on plate and keep warm in oven until all the omelets are completed.

1 To make filling, in medium skillet, heat o over medium-high heat until hot. Add onio and green pepper; cook until tender, about minutes. Add tomato and garlic; cook unt liquid has evaporated, about 2 to 3 minutes Add salt and red pepper flakes; set aside.

2 In small bowl, combine 3 eggs, 1 table spoon water and 1 tablespoon herbs until wel mixed. In 8-inch skillet, heat 1 tablespoon butter over medium-high heat until foamy Add egg mixture. Cook until egg starts to set about 30 seconds; gently stir until omelet ha set in large curds, about 1 to 2 minutes.

3 Place ¼ reserved filling on one side of omelet flip other side over filling to enclose. Holding handle, flip omelet onto plate.

4 Repeat with remaining filling mixture, eggs herbs and butter to make 3 more omelets.

Calories: 425 · Protein: 19 g
Fat: 35 g/ 75% Calories from Fat · Carbohydrate: 7g
Cholesterol: 853 mg · Sodium: 574 mg

Hoppin' John Salad

*Made with black-eyed peas, affectionately known as "cowpeas" in the South,
the classic Hoppin' John is traditionally served on New Year's Day for good luck in the coming year.*

erves 6

- CUP WATER
- ⁄2 CUP LONG-GRAIN RICE
- PACKAGE (10 OUNCES) FROZEN BLACK-EYED PEAS, THAWED
- TABLESPOONS LEMON JUICE
- TABLESPOON YELLOW MUSTARD
- CLOVE GARLIC, MINCED
- TEASPOONS GRATED LEMON PEEL (OPTIONAL)
- ⁄2 TEASPOON PEPPER
- ⁄3 CUP OLIVE OR OTHER VEGETABLE OIL
- PLUM TOMATOES, COARSELY CHOPPED
- RIBS CELERY, COARSELY CHOPPED
- LARGE YELLOW OR RED PEPPER, COARSELY CHOPPED
- GREEN ONIONS, COARSELY CHOPPED

1 In medium saucepan, combine water, rice and black-eyed peas over medium-high heat. Bring to a boil.

2 Reduce heat to medium-low; cover and simmer until rice and black-eyed peas are tender and liquid is absorbed, about 15 to 20 minutes.

3 Set aside saucepan and cool completely.

4 To make dressing, in small bowl, combine lemon juice, mustard, garlic, lemon peel, if desired, and pepper until well mixed. With fork, beat in oil.

5 In large serving bowl, combine black-eyed pea-rice mixture, chopped tomatoes, chopped celery, chopped yellow pepper, chopped onions and dressing; toss gently to evenly coat.

6 Serve at room temperature.

PREPARATION TIP

For timesaving planning, cook the rice and beans ahead and assemble before serving or even assemble the entire salad ahead to have on hand ready to eat.

Calories: 249 · Protein: 6 g
Fat: 13 g/ 46% Calories from Fat · Carbohydrate: 29 g
Cholesterol: 0 mg · Sodium: 60 mg

METRIC CONVERSIONS

DRY INGREDIENTS

Baking powder/soda	1 tsp. = 3 grams
Cornmeal	1 cup = 150 grams
Cornstarch	¼ cup = 30 grams
FLOUR	
All-purpose, unsifted	1 cup = 120 grams
Cake or pastry, sifted	1 cup = 100 grams
Whole-wheat, unsifted	1 cup = 125 grams
Nuts, coarsely chopped	1 cup = 140 grams
Herbs, dry	1 tsp. = 2 grams
Rice, uncooked	1 cup = 150 grams
Salt	1 tsp. = 5 grams
Spices, ground	1 tsp. = 2 grams
SUGAR	
Granulated	1 tsp. = 5 grams
	1 tbsp. = 15 grams
	1 cup = 200 grams
Confectioners'	1 cup = 110 grams
Brown, packed	1 cup = 220 grams

FATS, OILS, AND CHEESE

Butter	8 tablespoons =
	½ cup = 4 ounces =
	125 grams
Shortening or lard	1 cup = 250 grams
Vegetable oil	¼ cup = 60 ml
Cheese, grated	1 cup = 4 ounces =
	120 grams

LIQUID MEASURES

1 tablespoon	= 15 ml
1 fluid ounce	= 30 ml
¼ cup	= 60 ml
⅓ cup	= 80 ml
½ cup	= 125 ml
¾ cup	= 185 ml
1 cup	= 250 ml
1 quart	= 1 liter

WEIGHTS

1 ounce	= 30 grams
1 pound	= 450 grams
2.2 pounds	= 1 kilogram

FAHRENHEIT/CELSIUS CONVERSIONS

$9/5C + 32 = F$

$(F-32)5/9 = C$

OVEN TEMPERATURES

°Fahrenheit	°Celsius
250 (low oven)	120
300	150
325	160
350 (moderate oven)	175
400	200
450	230
500 (very hot oven)	260

INDEX

All-American Shrimp Salad, 50
apple(s)
  Butternut Soup, 75
  Kielbasa with Apples,
    Cabbage and Celery, 37
  Pork with Apple-Caraway Cream, 42
apricot(s)
  Chicken Breasts with
    Apricots and Almonds, 17
  Orange-Apricot Chicken Wings, 12
artichoke hearts
  Vegetable Antipasto Salad, 85
Asian-Style Tofu and Vegetables, 71
asparagus
  Pasta Primavera Salad, 69
  Spring Lamb and
    Asparagus Salad, 29
avocado
  California Chicken Salad with, 25
  Crab Louis, 64
  Lime Grilled Turkey Sandwiches, 21
  Spicy Tuna-Pasta Salad, 65

Beans, dried
  Asian-Style Tofu and Vegetables, 71
  Bean Burritos, 89
  Hoppin' John Salad, 91
  Modern Minestrone, 81
  Penne with Pepper,
    White Beans and Thyme, 74
  South-of-the-Border Black Bean
    Soup, 82
  Tomato-Vegetable Soup with
    Pesto, 70
  Two-Bean Salad, 88
  Vegetable Antipasto Salad, 85
beans, green
  French Potato Salad, 16
  Greek Green Bean Salad, 88
  Italian Beef Salad, 32
  Minted Chicken Salad, 23
  Spicy Lamb Sauté, 38
  Two-Bean Salad, 88
beef
  and Broccoli with
    Mustard Vinaigrette, 32
  burgers
    Cheese-Filled Pepper, 38
    Stovetop Barbecued, 36
  Italian Beef Salad, 32
  London Broil with
    Caramelized Onions, 36
  Microwave Baked Potato, 33
  Salisbury Steaks with
    Savory Sauce, 33
  Simple Beef Burgundy, 47

Spaghetti and Little Meatballs, 41
Spicy Fajita Roll-Ups, 45
broccoli
  Beef and, with
    Mustard Vinaigrette, 32
  Chicken Vegetable Stir-Fry, 20
  Fettucine with Green Vegetables, 82
  Linguine and, with Peanut Sauce, 75
  and Ricotta Pizza, 86
burgers
  Cheese-Filled Pepper, 38
  Herbed Turkey, 10
  Stovetop Barbecued, 36
Burritos, Bean, 89

Cabbage
  Kielbasa with Apples,
    Cabbage and Celery, 37
  Orange Chicken and
    Oriental Noodles, 27
  Pork and Linguine Stir-Fry, 44
Caesar Salad, Shrimp, 64
Calabacitas, 86
California Chicken Salad with
  Avocado, 25
cauliflower
  Spinach Pasta with
    Cauliflower-Cheddar Sauce, 80
cheese(s)
  Bean Burritos, 89
  Broccoli and Ricotta Pizza, 86
  Calabacitas, 86
  Cheese-Filled Pepper Burgers, 38
  Chicken Parmesan Sandwiches, 10
  Chicken Tortilla Soup, 8
  Devilish Drumsticks with
    Cheese Sauce, 15
  Fettucine with Green Vegetables, 82
  Greek Green Bean Salad, 88
  Minted Chicken Salad, 23
  Pesto with Linguine, 70
  Pork Parmesan, 30
  Radiatore Alla Norma, 78
  Spinach Pasta with
    Cauliflower-Cheddar Sauce, 80
  Two-Bean Salad, 88
  Vegetable Antipasto Salad, 85
chicken
  Breasts with
    Pineapple-Pepper Relish, 22
  Breasts with
    Apricots and Almonds, 17
  Chicken Parmesan Sandwiches, 10
  Devilish Drumsticks with
    Cheese Sauce, 15
  Orange, and Oriental Noodles, 27

Orange-Apricot Chicken Wings, 12
salads
  California Chicken, with
    Avocado, 25
  Chicken Noodle, 24
  French Potato, 16
  Minted Chicken, 23
  Moroccan Spiced Chicken, 13
soups and stews
  Chicken and Tiny Star Pasta
    Stew, 12
  Chicken Noodle, 9
  Hot-and-Sour Chicken Soup, 16
  Tortilla Soup, 8
  Spaghetti Primavera with, 25
stir-fry
  Chicken Vegetable, 20
  Spicy Chicken-Peanut, 18
Chinese Hot Pot, 42
corn
  Calabacitas, 86
  Chicken Noodle Soup, 9
  South-of-the-Border Black Bean
    Soup, 82
  Summer Turkey Salad, 9
Crab Louis, 64
curry
  Curried Zucchini Soup, 87
  Fish, 57

Devilish Drumsticks with
  Cheese Sauce, 15

Eggplant
  Radiatore Alla Norma, 78
  Shells with Pork Tenderloin and, 30
egg(s)
  Light Mushroom and
    Pepper Frittata, 76
  Spanish Omelet, 90

Fish and seafood. See seafood and fish
Fish Curry, 57
Foil-Baked Sole and Vegetables, 50
French Potato Salad, 16
Frittata, Light Mushroom and
  Pepper, 76

Gingered Turkey Kebabs, 7
Greek Green Bean Salad, 88
Grilled Salmon with Green Sauce, 49

Herb-Coated Salmon, 56
Herbed Turkey Burgers, 10
Honey-Thyme Turkey with
  Lemon Noodles, 22

ppin' John Salad, 91
t-and-Sour Chicken Soup, 16

lian Beef Salad, 32

oabs
Gingered Turkey, 7
wordfish Skewers with
  Garlic-Lime Marinade, 51
lbasa with Apples,
  Cabbage and Celery, 37

mb
picy Lamb Sauté, 38
pring Lamb and
  Asparagus Salad, 29
1on(s)
lounder with Lemon Cream, 69
Honey-Thyme Turkey with
  Lemon Noodles, 22
emon Turkey Scallops, 21
emony Spinach-Rice Soup, 72
ht Mushroom and
  Pepper Frittata, 76
ne Grilled Turkey Sandwiches, 21
e(s)
ime Grilled Turkey Sandwiches, 21
wordfish Skewers with
  Garlic-Lime Marinade, 51
Mein, Shrimp, 53
ndon Broil with
  Caramelized Onions, 36

crowave Baked Potato Stroganoff, 33
nestrone, Modern, 81
nted Chicken Salad, 23
dern Minestrone, 81
roccan Spiced Chicken Salad, 13
shroom(s)
Angel Hair Pasta with
  Veal, Mushrooms and Peas, 35
Chicken and Tiny Star Pasta Stew, 12
ight Mushroom and
  Pepper Frittata, 76
Microwave Baked Potato, 33
Noodles and, with
  Creamy Poppy Seed Sauce, 79
alisbury Steaks with
  Savory Sauce, 33
callop-Mushroom Noodle Soup, 59
imple Beef Burgundy, 47
wo-Bean Salad, 88

odles and Mushrooms with
Creamy Poppy Seed Sauce, 79

Omelet, Spanish, 90
onion(s)
  Calabacitas, 86
  Fettucine with Green Vegetables, 82
  London Broil with Caramelized, 36
  Spanish Omelet, 90
orange(s)
  Orange-Apricot Chicken Wings, 12
  Orange Chicken and
    Oriental Noodles, 27
  Orange Pork Stir-Fry, 45
  Red Snapper with Orange Sauce, 53
  Tuna-Spinach Salad, 60
Oriental Noodle Soup, 47

Paella Salad, 57
Parmesan Scallop Gratin, 61
pasta
  Angel Hair Pasta with
    Veal, Mushrooms and Peas, 35
  Fettuccine Alla Carbonara, 31
  Fettuccine with Fresh Salmon, 60
  Fettucine with Green Vegetables, 82
  Honey-Thyme Turkey with
    Lemon Noodles, 22
  Linguine and Broccoli with
    Peanut Sauce, 75
  Noodles and Mushrooms with
    Creamy Poppy Seed Sauce, 79
  Orange Chicken and
    Oriental Noodles, 27
  Penne with Pepper, White Beans
    and Thyme, 74
  Pesto with Linguine, 70
  Pork and Linguine Stir-Fry, 44
  Radiatore Alla Norma, 78
  Rotini with Flounder and
    Sun-Dried Tomato Pesto, 61
  salads
    Chicken Noodle Salad, 24
    Italian Beef Salad, 32
    Pasta Primavera Salad, 69
    Spicy Tuna-Pasta Salad, 65
    Summer Turkey, 9
  Shells with Pork Tenderloin and
    Eggplant, 30
  Shrimp Lo Mein, 53
  soups and stews
    Chicken and Tiny Star Pasta
      Stew, 12
    Chicken Noodle Soup, 9
    Oriental Noodle Soup, 47
    Scallop-Mushroom Noodle
      Soup, 59
    Turkey-Soba Soup, 15

Spaghetti and Little Meatballs, 41
Spaghetti Primavera with
  Chicken, 25
Spicy Lamb Sauté, 38
Spinach Pasta with
  Cauliflower-Cheddar Sauce, 80
peas
  Angel Hair Pasta with
    Veal, Mushrooms and, 35
  Asian-Style Tofu and Vegetables, 71
  Chicken Noodle Salad, 24
  Chinese Hot Pot, 42
  Fettucine with Green Vegetables, 82
  Pasta Primavera Salad, 69
  Pork and Linguine Stir-Fry, 44
  Scallop-Mushroom Noodle Soup, 59
Pecan-Crusted Snapper, 51
pepper(s)
  Calabacitas, 86
  Chicken Breasts with
    Pineapple-Pepper Relish, 22
  Light Mushroom and
    Pepper Frittata, 76
  Penne with Pepper, White Beans
    and Thyme, 74
  Spanish Omelet, 90
  Tomato-Pepper Topped Fish, 67
  Vegetable Antipasto Salad, 85
Pesto with Linguine, 70
Pizza, Broccoli and Ricotta, 86
pork
  with Apple-Caraway Cream, 42
  Fettuccine Alla Carbonara, 31
  Paella Salad, 57
  Parmesan, 30
  Pork Chops Diablo, 37
  Satay with Dipping Sauce, 40
  Shells with Pork Tenderloin and
Eggplant, 30
  soups and stews
    Chinese Hot Pot, 42
    Oriental Noodle Soup, 47
  Spaghetti and Little Meatballs, 41
  stir-fry
    Linguine and, 44
    Orange, 45
potato(es)
  All-American Shrimp Salad, 50
  Apple-Butternut Soup, 75
  Beef and Broccoli with Mustard
    Vinaigrette, 32
  Cakes, 81
  French Potato Salad, 16
  Microwave Baked Potato, 33
  Vegetable Antipasto Salad, 85

Rice
Hoppin' John Salad, 91
Lemony Spinach-Rice Soup, 72
Paella Salad, 57
Tuna-Rice Salad, 54

Salad(s)
All-American Shrimp, 50
California Chicken, with Avocado, 25
Chicken Noodle, 24
Cod, with Parsley Dressing, 65
Crab Louis, 64
French Potato, 16
Greek Green Bean, 88
Hoppin' John, 91
Italian Beef, 32
Minted Chicken, 23
Moroccan Spiced Chicken, 13
Paella, 57
Pasta Primavera, 69
Shrimp Caesar, 64
Spicy Tuna-Pasta, 65
Spring Lamb and Asparagus, 29
Summer Turkey, 9
Tuna-Rice, 54
Tuna-Spinach, 60
Two-Bean, 88
Vegetable Antipasto Salad, 85
Salisbury Steaks with Savory Sauce, 33
sandwich(es)
Chicken Parmesan, 10
Lime Grilled Turkey, 21
Satay, Pork, with Dipping Sauce, 40
sausage
Kielbasa with Apples,
Cabbage and Celery, 37
Sautéed Sesame Fish, 56
seafood and fish
All-American Shrimp Salad, 50
Cod Salad with Parsley Dressing, 65
Crab Louis, 64
Fettucine with Fresh Salmon, 60
Fish Curry, 57
Flounder with Lemon Cream, 59
Foil-Baked Sole and Vegetables, 50
Grilled Salmon with Green Sauce, 49
Herb-Coated Salmon, 56
Paella Salad, 57
Parmesan Scallop Gratin, 61
Pecan-Crusted Snapper, 51
Red Snapper with Orange Sauce, 53
Rotini with Flounder and Sun-Dried
Tomato Pesto, 61
Sautéed Sesame Fish, 56
Scallop-Mushroom Noodle Soup, 59

Shrimp Caesar Salad, 64
Shrimp Lo Mein, 53
Sole with Cucumber-Dill Sauce, 52
Spicy Tuna-Pasta Salad, 65
Swordfish Piccata, 62
Swordfish Skewers with
Garlic-Lime Marinade, 51
Tomato-Pepper Topped Fish, 67
Tuna-Rice Salad, 54
Tuna-Spinach Salad, 60
Simple Beef Burgundy, 47
soups and stews
Apple-Butternut Soup, 75
Chicken and Tiny Star Pasta Stew, 12
Chicken Noodle, 9
Chicken Tortilla, 8
Chinese Hot Pot, 42
Curried Zucchini, 87
Hot-and-Sour Chicken Soup, 16
Lemony Spinach-Rice, 72
Modern Minestrone, 81
Oriental Noodle Soup, 47
Scallop-Mushroom Noodle, 59
South-of-the-Border Black Bean
Soup, 82
Tomato-Vegetable Soup with
Pesto, 70
Turkey-Soba Soup, 15
South-of-the-Border Black Bean
Soup, 82
Spanish Omelet, 90
Spicy Chicken-Peanut Stir-Fry, 18
Spicy Fajita Roll-Ups, 45
Spicy Lamb Sauté, 38
Spicy Tuna-Pasta Salad, 65
spinach
Chicken Noodle Soup, 9
Fettucine with Green Vegetables, 82
Fish Curry, 57
Grilled Salmon with Green Sauce, 49
Lemony Spinach-Rice Soup, 72
Minted Chicken Salad, 23
Tuna-Spinach Salad, 60
Turkey-Soba Soup, 15
Spring Lamb and Asparagus Salad, 29
squash
Apple-Butternut Soup, 75
Tomato-Vegetable Soup with
Pesto, 70
stew. See soups and stews
stir-fry
Asian-Style Tofu and Vegetables, 71
Chicken Vegetable, 20
Orange Pork, 45
Pork and Linguine, 44

Spicy Chicken-Peanut, 18
Stovetop Barbecued Burgers, 36
Summer Turkey Salad, 9
Sweet-and-Sour Mustard Scallopini, 4
sweet potato(es)
Spring Lamb and
Asparagus Salad, 29

Tofu
Asian-Style Tofu and Vegetables, 71
Chinese Hot Pot, 42
tomato(es)
Chicken Tortilla Soup, 8
Modern Minestrone, 81
Radiatore Alla Norma, 78
Rotini with Flounder and
Sun-Dried Tomato Pesto, 61
Shells with Pork Tenderloin and
Eggplant, 30
Spaghetti and Little Meatballs, 41
Spanish Omelet, 90
Tomato-Pepper Topped Fish, 67
Tomato-Vegetable Soup with
Pesto, 70
turkey
Gingered Turkey Kebabs, 7
Herbed Turkey Burgers, 10
Honey-Thyme Turkey with
Lemon Noodles, 22
Lemon Turkey Scallops, 21
Lime Grilled Turkey Sandwiches, 2
Soba Soup, 15
Summer Turkey Salad, 9
Two-Bean Salad, 88

Veal
Angel Hair Pasta with
Veal, Mushrooms and Peas, 35
Sweet-and-Sour Mustard
Scallopini, 40
Vegetable Antipasto Salad, 85

Zucchini
Calabacitas, 86
Curried Zucchini Soup, 87
Oriental Noodle Soup, 47
Tomato-Vegetable Soup with
Pesto, 70